Comments on other *Amazing Stories* from readers & reviewers

*"You might call them the non-fiction response to Harlequin
romances: easy to consume and potentially addictive."*
Robert Martin, *The Chronicle Herald*

*"Tightly written volumes filled with lots of wit and humour
about famous and infamous Canadians."*
Eric Shackleton, *The Globe and Mail*

*"This is popular history as it should be …
For this price, buy two and give one to a friend."*
Terry Cook, a reader from Ottawa, on **Rebel Women**

*"Stories are rich in description, and
bristle with a clever, stylish realness."*
Mark Weber, *Central Alberta Advisor,* on **Ghost Town Stories II**

*"The resulting book is one readers will want
to share with all the women in their lives."*
Lynn Martel, *Rocky Mountain Outlook,* on **Women Explorers**

"[The books are] *long on plot and character and short
on the sort of technical analysis that can be dreary
for all but the most committed academic."*
Robert Martin, *The Chronicle Herald*

*"A compelling read. Bertin … has selected only the most intriguing
tales, which she narrates with a wealth of detail."*
Joyce Glasner, *New Brunswick Reader,* on **Strange Events**

*"The heightened sense of drama and intrigue, combined with a
good dose of human interest is what sets* Amazing Stories *apart."*
Pamela Klaffke, *Calgary Herald*

CANADIANS ON EVEREST

AMAZING STORIES®

CANADIANS ON EVEREST

The Courageous Expedition of 1982

BRUCE PATTERSON

PUBLISHED BY ALTITUDE PUBLISHING CANADA LTD.
1500 Railway Avenue, Canmore, Alberta T1W 1P6
www.altitudepublishing.com
www.amazingstories.ca
1-800-957-6888

Extreme care has been taken to ensure that all information presented in
this book is accurate and up to date. Neither the author nor the
publisher can be held responsible for any errors.

Publisher	Stephen Hutchings
Series Editor	Diana Marshall
Editor	Jill Foran
Cover and layout	Zoe Howes

We acknowledge the financial support of the Government
of Canada through the Book Publishing Industry Development
Program (BPIDP) for our publishing activities.

Altitude GreenTree Program
Altitude Publishing will plant twice as many trees as were used
in the manufacturing of this product.

Library And Archives of Canada Cataloguing in Publication Data

Patterson, Bruce
    Canadians on Everest / Bruce Patterson.

ISBN 1-55439-234-9

    1. Canadian Mount Everest Expedition (1982) 2. Mountaineering--Everest, Mount (China and Nepal)
3. Mountaineers--Canada. 4. Everest, Mount (China and Nepal)--Description and travel.
I. Title. II. Series: Amazing stories (Calgary, Alta.)

GV199.44.E85P38 2006   796.522095496   C2006-906163-7

Amazing Stories® is a registered trademark of Altitude Publishing Canada Ltd.

For general information on Altitude Publishing and the Amazing Stories, including all books published by
Altitude Publishing, please call our order line at 1-800-957-6888. For reseller information, including discounts
and premium sales, please call our sales department at 403-678-9592. For press review copies, author
interviews, or other publicity information, please contact our marketing department at 403-283-7934, or via
fax at 403-283-7917. For general information, visit our Web sites: *www.amazingstories.ca* and
www.altitudepublishing.com

Printed and bound in Canada by Friesens
2 4 6 8 9 7 5 3 1

To Joan Wagner, for her courageous, loving, and adventurous spirit.

Contents

Prologue

Laurie Skreslet stood at the edge of the gaping crevasse and faced an agonizing decision. He was in the Khumbu Icefall, one of the most dangerous mountaineering environments on the earth. And he was alone. Farther up the mountain, on the other side of the chasm, his teammates were pushing a route toward the summit of the Himalayan giant.

Laurie was in pain. His broken ribs still hadn't healed from the six-metre fall he'd suffered earlier in the expedition. He desperately wanted to join the other climbers, but he knew the risk was perilous.

A makeshift bridge of ropes and an aluminum ladder had provided safe passage for those who had already crossed the 30-metre-deep gap. But the constantly shifting maze of ice and snow that spills down the flank of Everest had pulled the ladder loose. Laurie searched in vain for an alternate route, but he soon realized that if he wanted to continue, he would have to make a 1.5-metre jump from the end of the ladder to a precarious ledge on the other side.

There was no shame in turning back. Leader Bill March had already made it clear that he thought it was too dangerous for Laurie to even attempt climbing through the icefall on his own. Not only was there still the risk of avalanche, but seracs (towering blocks of ice) could collapse at any time. And yawning crevasses could shift or open up in an instant. It was Russian roulette for those who dared to claw their way up or around the frozen pillars stacked at every conceivable angle.

If Laurie were climbing with others, there would at least be a chance of rescue if he fell and injured himself. But alone, there was only a remote chance he would come out alive. His ribs throbbed as he thought of the damage already inflicted on his body. Would he survive a second fall? He was in radio contact with mountaineers spread out in camps up and down the mountain, but this was a test of self-reliance. Laurie knew his progress reports to base camp were serving one primary purpose — to make it easier for the team to find his body if he failed to make it through.

Taking one last look at the crevasse in front of him, Laurie decided that he'd given his best effort on the mountain. But as he prepared to retreat to the safety of base camp, a nagging doubt remained. Was there more he could give?

The jump looked impossible, but he had to try. Pushing his fear to the back of his mind, he secured the safety ropes as best he could and pounded anchors into the snow. He then attached clamps to the lines that would hopefully minimize the damage if he fell into the icy chasm.

"At best, the odds are 50-50 that I'll make it," he told himself as he edged his way out to the end of the ladder and made his leap.

Chapter 1
Bold Ambition

Bill March looked around at the climbers gathered in the lecture room at the University of Calgary (U of C) and said, in his typically direct style, "If there are deaths on the mountain, we will continue as long as it is safe and practical to do so."

It was the spring of 1982. The mountain he was talking about was Everest, and we were preparing to climb it — Canada's first expedition to the world's highest peak.

Bill's words sounded theoretical in the campus setting, but the team had already received a stark reminder that mountaineering comes with a deadly risk. Just a few months earlier, John Lauchlan, one of the youngest members of the group, had gone out to scale a steep series of frozen waterfalls draped down the side of Cirrus Mountain along the Banff-Jasper Parkway. John was among the most daring of the modern generation of climbers who used specialized hand tools with high-angled picks to scale vertical and overhanging pitches of ice.

An instructor at the Yamnuska Mountain School on the eastern edge of the Rockies, John thrived on being at the leading edge. Most ice climbers travel in pairs or groups and use safety ropes and large hollow metal screws to anchor themselves to the ice in case of a fall. John was among the few who are skilled and experienced enough to go out on their own. While these elite climbers carry ropes to guard themselves on the most serious parts of a route, they often leave those lifelines in their packs, choosing instead to operate like tightrope walkers without a net. They must rely solely on their skills and concentration in order to succeed and survive, and this lifts the endeavour to a whole new level of intensity. The greater risk, the greater the reward. "Go big or go home," was John's credo.

The 27-year-old was determined to become the first climber to solo a difficult route on Cirrus Mountain known as Polar Circus. He'd gone out several times to make the attempt, but had always pulled back. Sometimes, the mountain hadn't felt right. Other times, he hadn't felt right. As he prepared to head out for another attempt on the morning of February 5, 1982, John assured his wife, Mary, that this time would be no different. He wouldn't push too hard.

John was as confident and cautious as ever when he began his climb. Moving quickly and with the efficiency of a lone traveller, he ascended the first two falls of the Polar Circus route in a couple of hours. He had to cross a potentially dangerous snow slope to get to the next series of falls, but he could reduce the risk of triggering a slide by staying close to rocks on the edge of the snow. He had just about reached solid ground when a small slab broke loose beneath his feet.

In an instant, John was swept down the mountain face. The blast of the avalanche sent the helpless mountaineer over a 20-metre cliff. From tracks in the snow, it appeared that John had survived that first fall but had felt that his injury was too serious to wait for others to find him. In an attempt to make it back to the road, he had rigged a rope system to lower himself down over the lower waterfall, and he had tentatively begun the descent. In the end, he just didn't have the strength to hang on any longer. It was 1 a.m. when Jim Elzinga, another member of the Everest team, found John's body at the base of the falls.

Although the loss of his friend hit him hard, Jim remained on the Everest expedition. And he didn't need Bill March to remind him about the high stakes of the climb. For Jim, who began climbing while in high school in Calgary, there was no question about the rewards of experiencing life in its fullest sense, whether in the mountains or anywhere else. He was articulate about the appeal of mountain adventure: "We grow up in a society where, from the time we're born, there are support mechanisms around us. When you're a little baby, your mother and father take care of you. When you grow up a little bit, you go to school. Everyone's either taking care of you or telling you what to do. This human safety net is created around you and I don't think most people realize this net is there. When I go climbing, I remove myself from that human safety net. I remove myself from all those outside constraints that I perceive, whether they be real or real in my own mind. The challenge is within myself. Whether I'm successful, the only person who's really going to care about that is me. Whether I do that hard move, that's my challenge. At times, those challenges stress you along that fine line between victory and death. Sometimes you have a foot on either side. There's something that drives you to push a little harder. It's in tapping into that source that I get immense satisfaction. In nothing else I've ever done have I been able to tap into that."

While Jim and John were ambitious climbers, both had initially held reservations about joining the Canadian Mount Everest Expedition. Organizers were planning a traditional siege-style ascent, with a large team using Sherpas for support and oxygen tanks to help cope with the altitude. For the young climbers, this represented an old-school approach that was developed back in the days when expeditions were run like military assaults and teams relied on the strength of numbers to push their way up through hostile terrain. The strategy called for climbers to establish a series of camps up the mountain, linked by several kilometres of fixed ropes. A fortified supply route was to extend to the upper reaches of the mountain, where a small summit team would finally push for the top. The siege-style technique increases the chances of success, but the trade-off is that the climb is less challenging, and therefore less rewarding when the goal is accomplished.

The expedition's intended route — through the maze of the Khumbu Icefall, up the avalanche-prone gap between Everest and its sister peak, Lhotse, then on to the South Col and eventually the summit — was another bone of contention for the young, independent climbers. This route was the most commonly attempted way to tackle the mountain. Sir Edmund Hillary had climbed it with Tenzing Norgay in 1953. In the ensuing years, more than 100 people had scaled the mountain, and many of these climbers had increased the challenge by tackling steeper and more technically difficult terrain. While Jim and John would have preferred a more daring approach, the pair eventually signed on with the Canadian expedition. Soon after, they began to lobby the rest of the team to alter the route to include the ascent of a difficult unclimbed rock face and earn the right to name it the "Canadian Spur." This was John's way of adding the "go big" element to the challenge — to veer off the terrain where others had already succeeded and achieve a unique accomplishment for Canadian climbing.

Sadly, John wouldn't get the chance to push the envelope on Everest, and his death marked a significant shift in the atmosphere surrounding preparations for the expedition. They took on a new air of solemnity.

The attempt was set to begin in July 1982, but there had already been close to five years' work on the project. During those years, the great adventure had been sidetracked a number of times by disputes over sponsorship and leadership, and by personality clashes among team members. Indeed, it often seemed that the logistics of the enterprise would overwhelm the essential elements of personal challenge and the struggle to survive and succeed on the world's tallest mountain.

Everest has held a singular attraction for mountaineers since 1852, when the Great Trigonometrical Survey of India revealed that a massive black pyramid known simply as Peak XV had the distinction of being the highest point on the earth. At first, surveyors thought it was 8840 metres, but calculations carried out in the 1950s established the commonly accepted measure of 8848 metres. In recent years, new techniques involving satellite technology have set the height at some 8850 metres.

In the fashion of the old British Empire, the peak was named in 1865 in honour of Sir George Everest, the superintendent of the Survey of India who had spent 25 years charting the terrain that spanned 2400 kilometres of the subcontinent. It didn't matter at the time to the western world that the Sherpas who lived on the upper reaches of the Himalayas had their own name for the majestic peak — *Chomolungma,* or "Mother Goddess of the Earth."

Bold Ambition

Mountaineers began to consider seriously the possibility of scaling Everest in the early 1900s, but the challenges were daunting. There were fears that even with the development of oxygen tanks and breathing masks, humans might not be able to survive at extreme altitude. And, at that time, both Tibet and Nepal had tight restrictions on foreign visitors.

In the early 1920s, British adventurers, with the aid of the Dalai Lama, managed to secure permission for a series of expeditions on the Tibetan side of the peak. George Leigh Mallory emerged as a driving force in the quest. Mallory was well known for his succinct answer when asked why he wanted to climb Everest: "Because it's there."

He also had a more eloquent explanation: "If you cannot understand that there is something in man which responds to the challenge of this mountain and goes out to meet it, that the struggle is the struggle of life itself upward and forever upward, then you won't see why we go. What we get from this adventure is just sheer joy. And joy is, after all, the end of life. We do not live to eat and make money. We eat and make money to be able to enjoy life. That is what life means and what life is for."

In 1924, after two previous attempts at the mountain, Mallory embarked on his third and final Everest expedition. He would soon be at the centre of one of the most intriguing mysteries of the mountaineering world. By early June, Mallory and his climbing companion, Andrew Irvine, had pushed a route beyond 8000 metres on the North Face. The pair was spotted pushing for the top on the Northeast Ridge.

They were just 300 metres below their lofty goal when they were last seen alive. Their bodies were not recovered by their teammates, and the question soon emerged: Did they reach the top before they perished? While Mallory's remains were eventually found in 1999, the question remains unanswered.

There were repeated attempts at the summit in the years leading up to World War II, with British climbers still at the forefront. In 1952, a Swiss expedition came tantalizingly close to the top, but the mountain, with its volatile wind and snowstorms, proved too much of a challenge.

It was May 29, 1953, when, beyond doubt, the "Third Pole" was finally reached. The attention of the world was focused on a young Princess Elizabeth, who had just been crowned Queen of England. Far from the pomp and circumstance, Colonel John Hunt was leading yet another British expedition to Everest. In the wake of the 1949 Chinese revolution, Tibet had been cut off, and foreigners were forced to approach the peak through Nepal. After a 17-day trek to the base of Everest, the expedition began probing a route through the foreboding Khumbu Icefall. For the next six weeks, climbers and Sherpas hauled gear and established nine camps up the mountainside. On May 21, it looked like the mountain would once again prove too daunting when a pair of exhausted would-be summiteers turned back. The hopes of the team fell on the shoulders of a second pair, a New Zealand beekeeper named Edmund Hillary and his Sherpa climbing partner, Tenzing Norgay. After five hours of climbing into the unknown with bulky oxygen tanks and rudimentary climbing gear, Hillary and Norgay reached the top. "The whole world spread out below us," Hillary later said.

After the success of the British team in 1953, more climbers soon matched the feat, with Swiss, Americans, Italians, and others swelling the ranks of Everest summiteers. Canadians were still almost 30 years away from joining them. Mountain climbing was practised by a select few in Western Canada. While there had been some little-known successful climbs by Canadians in the Himalayas, there was a feeling among some climbers that Canada was long overdue for an attempt on Everest.

"It's a bloody outrage," British-born adventurer Roger Marshall told me at a pub in Golden, British Columbia, as he slammed his beer mug on the table for emphasis. I had arranged to meet the burly climber at the Mad Trapper for a beer and some background information on his bold plan to forge a Canadian expedition to the top of the world.

A newspaper reporter turned building contractor, Roger had started out as a working-class climber in the Lake District of England. During the counterculture era of the 1960s and 1970s, the rebellious approach to everything from fashion to politics had pervaded the climbing world. And while this anti-authoritarian approach to climbing England's cliffs and crags was a far cry from the traditional regimented style of British mountaineering, it suited Roger. "We were all dead anti-social," he recalled. "On climbing trips we would sleep in barns. We'd drink hard but we'd climb hard."

As a new Canadian, Roger seemed to take it as a personal insult that many other countries had succeeded in sending teams to Everest while his adopted country had not. He decided to do something about it and organize his own expedition. This meant having to practically browbeat the Alpine Club of Canada's expedition committee into endorsing his proposal. He eventually won their support, and in 1978, the Nepalese government granted him a climbing permit for the post-monsoon season of 1982.

At first, Roger wanted to keep the expedition relatively small and low-key in terms of Everest attempts, with a budget of about $100,000. But by the time he received formal permission, his vision of a small-scale expedition was fading. And, almost from the beginning, the seeds of dissension that would cause so many problems on the mountain were already being sewn.

Roger found the core of his Everest team among a loose-knit group of climbers that he'd assembled to summit Alaska's Mount McKinley in 1977. Called the CLOD Expedition — Calgary Leftovers Outing to Denali (the traditional native name for McKinley) — the McKinley climb had been a success; all eight members of the team had made it to the top. Among them was a young climber from Kimberley, British Columbia, named Pat Morrow, and a pair who, like Roger, were transplanted from England — Dave Read of Calgary and Gordon "Speedy" Smith of Golden.

When Roger invited the members of the CLOD

Expedition to join the Everest team, Pat Morrow jumped at the chance, although he had trouble focusing on an adventure that was still four years down the road. The freelance photographer had more immediate concerns as he pursued a nomadic lifestyle roaming the mountains in a well-used van and taking vivid images of the wilderness. Dave Read, a millwright who worked in northern Alberta's oil industry when the need arose, was also intrigued by the prospect of Everest. He had been part of the climbing counterculture both in England and in Calgary and relished the idea of a grand and glorious holiday. "We only pass this way but once, mate. You've got to have a bit of fun," the climber liked to say. By the early 1980s, he had given up the security of his trade to open the Easy Street Rockers climbing shop in Vancouver.

As the team began to take shape, many of Canada's best mountaineers lobbied to join, and early members voted on additions based on the strengths the "applicants" could offer. Gordon Smith's wife, Marlene, another climbing friend of Roger's from Golden, was among the first climbers asked to join the expedition. Marlene was to be the only woman in the group, but as power struggles began to erupt and the demands of organizing the attempt grew, she dropped off the team. Don Serl, a Vancouver mountain equipment store manager and respected West Coast climber, was also an early recruit. Three instructors in the outdoor pursuits program at the U of C — George Kinnear, Rusty Baillie, and Bill March — were added as well.

All approaching 40, the trio of mountaineers from the university added an element of maturity to the team. They shared an academic and analytical approach to climbing, but each had his own special area of focus. George Kinnear was a specialist in the physical aspects of climbing. He studied the effects of high altitude on the body and the body's response to the rigours of the sport. Bill March was interested in climbing as part of the tradition of adventure. He could quote revered mountaineers and expound on the need for challenge in modern society. He would analyze distinct aspects of an adventure from the preliminary stages of anticipation, to the event itself, to the time of reflection and introspection that came afterward. Rusty Baillie had an esoteric approach to climbing, and he studied its spiritual side. He planned to use the expedition as part of his doctoral research on meditation and other mental techniques in mountaineering.

The U of C climbers gave the team credibility, but they had little in common with the man who had launched the expedition. Roger's leadership came into question as soon as the team began taking a hard look at the years of organization and fundraising that would be required to finance the attempt. The climbers knew they needed a professional approach that would get them into the boardrooms of Canadian corporations and a salesman with a diplomatic touch to enlist a broad base of support. They had serious doubts that Roger was their man.

Only a few months after formal approval was granted for the expedition, Roger was voted out as leader. George

Kinnear was given the job of putting the expedition together, with the added challenge of dealing with Roger as his deputy. In the four years leading up to our departure for the mountain, the team underwent incredible changes. Some climbers were added for their special knowledge and Himalayan experience. Banff warden Tim Auger and Canmore alpine safety specialist Lloyd "Kiwi" Gallagher were invited to join the group because they had been on the first Canadian team to achieve a major success in the Himalayas. Their 1977 ascent of Mount Pumori had given them magnificent and tantalizing views of Everest, looming across a glacier-lined valley.

John Amatt, who was running management programs and wilderness seminars at The Banff Centre, was added as a climber and quickly assumed the role of business manager. A huge corporate structure began to evolve, with all the trappings of a modern business — flow charts, a board of directors, an expedition lawyer, and a six-page climber's contract. For those who bothered to read that agreement, the equivalent of a morality clause was contained in section 13. It gave the team the right to kick a member off the climb if he did anything to "tarnish" his reputation and jeopardize the expedition.

In October 1979, the *Calgary Herald* and Southam News jointly bought the newspaper rights for the expedition story for $25,000. As the *Herald*'s bureau reporter stationed in the Rockies, I was chosen to cover the climb. This meant learning the basics of mountaineering so that I could accompany the team to a high-altitude camp where I would relay stories back to Canada. John Lauchlan had already taught me the basics of rock climbing, as I had spent some time training with him earlier that year at the Yamnuska Mountain School. Prior to this, however, my view of climbing had been very narrow. I'd seen it as nothing more than a high-risk pursuit that offered intangible rewards for those who could claw their way up sheer rock walls or frozen cliffs using ropes and an assortment of specialized devices. I had written about several climbing fatalities and held little appreciation for the skills that climbers develop to protect themselves in hazardous terrain. But that changed in the summer of 1979, when I climbed a moderate route on Mount Yamnuska with John and got a taste of the exhilaration that comes after scaling a towering rock wall, gazing out at spectacular vistas, and feeling the satisfaction of overcoming physical challenges and fear.

In December 1980, I joined Bill March, Rusty Baillie, and George Kinnear, along with a group of climbing students, for an ascent of Cotopaxi, a 5975-metre volcano in Ecuador. The South American peak is more than 2000 metres higher than Mount Robson, the highest point in the Canadian Rockies, and I soon discovered what it's like to function at heights where the oxygen level gets thinner and thinner. Breathing is more laboured and headaches are common. With the risk of fluids accumulating in the lungs or brain, altitude sickness can be fatal. Our group learned that a "bell-ringer" — a throbbing head pain to rival the worst hangover — is a signal to get down to lower elevation immediately. We followed the basic precautions of drinking as much water as we could and taking time to gradually acclimatize to the rarefied air.

After several days of instruction, I began to get comfortable with climbing on the frozen terrain using crampons on my boots for traction and an ice axe for stability. When it was finally time to put my new skills to the test and go for the summit, I was ready. I felt confident as I started up the mountainside before dawn. Hours later, that confidence was pushed aside by growing doubts. I reminded myself of the key to success on a big mountain: just keep putting one foot in front of the other. Lines from Pink Floyd's "Another Brick in the Wall" began to drift through my consciousness — "We don't need no education. We don't need no thought control." Not a positive sentiment, but it helped me maintain a rhythm as I plodded upward.

The climb was a bit of an emotional roller coaster; I would feel a sense of accomplishment when I could see how far I'd come, then a sense of frustration after reaching a "false summit" — an apparition that appeared to be the top until I reached it and it became clear how much more mountain there was to climb. On the brink of exhaustion, I was caught off guard when Bill March, who was just ahead of me on the rope, turned and said, "Go ahead, this is your summit." Suddenly we were on the rim of the volcano, basking in the bright morning sunshine high above the broken cloud cover. Tears welled up as I looked out at the vast Ecuadorian plains and felt a deep sense of satisfaction. Like a runner who had completed a marathon, I was physically drained but eager to take on another challenge — to face another test with a new sense of confidence.

As I continued with my own preparations, other team members embarked on an ambitious plan to gain high-altitude experience before tackling Everest. In 1981, several members of the expedition attempted an ascent of Nuptse, one of Everest's sister peaks. Jim Elzinga led the team that planned the ascent of the daunting South Face of the 7789-metre peak. He was joined by Bill March, Rusty Baillie, and John Lauchlan, as well as three climbers who taught with Lauchlan at the Yamnuska Mountain School — Dwayne Congdon, James Blench, and Dave McNab. The team was rounded out by Calgary climber Laurie Skreslet, who was also an instructor with Outward Bound, an outdoor challenge program that aims to instil people with confidence in their own capabilities and trust in working with others.

The members of the Nuptse expedition got a vivid idea of some of the challenges and dangers they would face the following year. Reaching the base of Nuptse required the same approach march through leech-infested terrain that the Everest expedition would soon have to endure. But the challenges didn't stop there. Before their "rehearsal" expedition was over, the climbers would also receive a sobering reminder of the awesome forces at work in the Himalayas.

From the start, the Nuptse team had to exercise extreme caution. Their original route was abandoned because of high avalanche danger. They then backed off an alternate route because of treacherous rockfall. A new line was planned up the South Buttress and on to the West Ridge. Finally, confident they had found the best route, the team quickly pushed up the mountainside and fixed more than one kilometre of rope as they ascended to the 6550-metre level.

The elements soon threw up another obstacle. A fierce storm hit the mountain and packed the slopes with heavy snow. The climbers retreated. On their hasty descent, they considered stopping at advance camp to wait out the storm. Despite some opposition, Jim insisted they return to their base lower on the mountain, as it would offer more security and comfort if they were stalled for an extended period. The storm broke quickly, however, and the team returned to their advance camp the following day.

They were astounded by the scene that greeted them. The spot where their camp had been was now a huge mound of boulders. Their tents, where they had considered staying to wait out the storm, were now under 10 metres of rubble. Each man knew that if the group had slept in their high camp, they wouldn't have had a chance.

Though shaken by the unpredictable nature of the slide, a few of the team members were determined to make another attempt at the summit. But, after a tentative probe back up the mountain, they realized they had lost too much food and equipment. Reluctantly, they conceded defeat and began the long journey home.

Bill March was ready to quit the Everest attempt. "There's no way I'm coming back," he said over and over again in a trekking lodge as he swigged a combination of Star beer, chang (rice beer), and brandy.

Back in Canada, Bill continued to examine his own willingness to face the risks of the Himalayas again. He talked it over with his wife, Karen, and reflected on the effort he had already put into the expedition. He took time to weigh his decision.

"The greatest hazard to life is to risk nothing," reads an anonymous quote in a collection of philosophical notes Bill had gathered over the years. "The man who risks nothing, does nothing, has nothing, is nothing. He may avoid suffering but he simply cannot learn, feel, change, grow, love, live."

Bill decided to stay on the team. Within three months, he was named its new leader, replacing George Kinnear, who resigned after suffering an eye hemorrhage during a training climb. Bill seemed to have the right combination of Himalayan experience, public relations skills, and bravado that was needed to deal with the strong-willed individuals who were being brought together for the historic undertaking.

While both men were British-born, Bill had a much different approach to mountaineering than Roger. Educated at King's College, London, he combined his climbing exploits with an academic career and served as director of the National Mountaineering School in Britain before immigrating to Canada. He could drink and sing bawdy mountaineering songs with the best of them, but as he left his university days behind, he was also cautious about letting rowdy nights get out of hand. Bill took his new job as team leader very seriously, heeding advice offered by Machiavelli centuries earlier: "There are few things more difficult to take in hand, more perilous to conduct or more uncertain in their success than to accept the responsibilities for providing leadership."

While the Canadian Everest team and its organizational structure had grown, so had its budget. Roger Marshall's original plans for a $100,000 attempt were long gone. The projected costs had soared past $500,000 and were well on their way to $1 million. John Amatt's promotional skills had paid off, however, and Air Canada had signed on as the official sponsor of the expedition.

The final months of preparation were hectic as members tackled an array of chores. Base camp manager Peter Spear, a Calgary high school vice principal, enlisted a small army of volunteers to pack food. Meanwhile, Laurie Skreslet and Jim Elzinga were busy advising equipment manufacturers on the design of heavy-duty down-filled parkas and sleeping bags. Laurie was also working on the production of specialized tents that featured telescoping legs (for perching on steep mountain slopes) and a shell of bulletproof fabric (to deflect falling rocks and ice). The shell looked like the canopy of a chuckwagon, but Laurie, who grew up just a few blocks from the Calgary Stampede grounds, insisted it was just a coincidence.

Even in those final months, the team continued to grow and change in character. Kurt Fuhrich, a Banff restaurateur and veteran world-traveller, signed on as camp cook with the promise of gourmet meals on the mountain. Dave Jones, a British-born mountaineer with experience working in remote oil regions, joined as base camp doctor. Another physician, University of Toronto graduate Steve Bezruchka, who had worked on medical aid projects in Nepal and written a guidebook for the country, enlisted as the team's high-altitude doctor.

While Jim Elzinga was off ferrying a load of supplies overland to Kathmandu, team leaders invited Alan Burgess to join the expedition. He and his twin brother, Adrian, had extensive Himalayan experience, and the decision to add Alan to the group seemed like a good one. However, it would soon prove to be a sore point that further strained relationships among various team members.

Jim and Alan — both big, powerful, and determined climbers — had achieved some notable successes together in previous years. Their finest accomplishment had been on Mount Logan in 1979. The team had spent 16 days on Canada's highest mountain and had made the first ascent of the 6050-metre peak's Southwest Buttress. But in 1981, when they joined forces again for an attempt of the 8167-metre Dhaulagiri, things were much different. John Lauchlan was kicked off the expedition for no apparent reason — at least as far as Jim could see. Jim had remained on the team, but he'd felt very much like the odd man out. The isolation was worse higher up the mountain where the Burgess twins kept to themselves and ultimately reached the summit. The hard feelings from the Dhaulagiri trip were far from reconciled when Alan was asked to join the Everest expedition.

Despite the requirement that all team members be Canadian or landed immigrants — Adrian Burgess was excluded from consideration because he had settled in Boulder, Colorado — there was a diverse array of accents among the climbers gathered under a single flag. Lloyd "Kiwi" Gallagher, who was from New Zealand, joked about all the $10 Canadians on the team, referring to the ones who had paid for citizenship papers. Rusty Baillie came from Africa via Outward Bound in Colorado. And John Amatt, Bill March, Roger Marshall, Dave Read, Alan Burgess, and Gordon Smith were from Britain. The home-grown climbers included Jim Elzinga, Pat Morrow, Laurie Skreslet, Don Serl, Tim Auger, Dave McNab, James Blench, and Dwayne Congdon.

In all, there were 16 climbers on the team. It was not a harmonious group, but momentum was building and the hard feelings and political manoeuvrings subsided as the climbers began to focus on the mountain and its hazards.

Meanwhile, my own role on the expedition was evolving. After the climb in Ecuador, Bill March was satisfied that I could handle myself on Everest. He told me that I was welcome to go beyond base camp if I wanted to, but that I'd be expected to haul loads up the mountainside just like the others. It was an amazing opportunity and I readily agreed, eager to be as close to the action as possible.

I was full of optimism that summer. On July 14, three days before the expedition was set to leave, I married my sweetheart, Joan Wagner, on the banks of the Bow River in Banff. I was 32 years old and full of confidence as I looked to the future. But I wasn't ignoring the risks ahead. Like other members of the expedition, I wrote my will before leaving Canada.

Chapter 2
Send-off and Setbacks

Bill March reached under his shirt, pulled a thick wad of American bills from a bulky money belt, and handed me $5000 across the aisle of the jetliner. "Hold this for me until we get through customs," he said, then proceeded to distribute more packets of cash to other members of the expedition.

We were approaching Seattle, and American regulations prohibited carrying more than $5000 into the country. It was mid-morning, Saturday, July 17, 1982. After years of planning and a long series of changes in personnel, we were finally on our way.

One member of the team had joined the expedition so late that I didn't meet him until we were on the plane. Blair

Griffiths, a Vancouver cameraman and climber, had been enlisted to shoot videotape during the long trek to Everest and then follow the team's progress as far as possible up the mountainside. Expedition organizers had clinched a last-minute deal with the Canadian Broadcasting Corporation (CBC) to provide television coverage for the network's week-end sports programming and its recently launched nightly news package, *The National* and *The Journal*. The CBC was enticed by the prospect of providing the first live television coverage of mountaineers reaching the summit of Everest. It was an ambitious plan because it meant relaying and trans-mitting signals from a remote part of a Third World country that didn't have a television service of its own.

To carry out the plan, the CBC commandeered the top floor of the Everest Sheraton in Kathmandu and installed a $500,000 production studio. Teleglobe Canada, meanwhile, spent close to $1.8 million on construction of an earth sta-tion at the hotel. The earth station would beam signals into space, and these signals would be relayed by three satel-lites to transmit the expedition images to Canadian homes. Team members would shoot videotape footage during the early stages of the climb, with Sherpa runners carrying the material back to Kathmandu. Later, a state-of-the-art video camera would be used high on the mountain. It would relay a signal to a series of temporary microwave towers strung 240 kilometres from the heart of the Himalayas through rhodo-dendron forests and over deep river valleys to the capital. As a backup, a 12,000-millimetre telephoto lens would be trained on the mountain from the Everest View Hotel, near Namche Bazaar, 25 kilometres away.

The expedition had grown into a $3-million enterprise. Air Canada was spending close to $1 million in sponsorship and promotion, and a long list of other corporations had signed on as backers as well. We had $150,000 worth of Leica cameras and all the Kodak film we could use. A computerized system was established in Montreal to identify up to 36,000 photographs taken during the three-month adventure. We were also issued Hitachi stereo tape players and recorders called Perdiscos, as in "personal discos" (a reflection of the times), and climbing suits from Sun Ice. Mountaineers who tended to wear highly individualistic and sometimes motley attire while out on their own were garishly decked out in bright red and grey uniforms adorned with corporate logos. It seemed like "The Big Red Machine" from Canada was so well endowed with equipment and backup support that a mere mountain would pose an embarrassingly small challenge.

From the start of our journey, however, it was apparent that the best-laid plans can indeed go awry. We hadn't even left North America when we hit the first snag. Our trek to the other side of the world began with a short flight from Vancouver to Seattle, where we would board a 747 headed for Bangkok, Thailand. But we had barely touched down on the tarmac in Seattle when the captain turned on the intercom and told us to get ready for a long wait. Refugees from Southeast Asia, in the lengthy wake of the Vietnam War, had arrived just ahead of us on two jumbo jets and all other international traffic was held up while the Vietnamese went through the laborious process of filing through American customs and immigration. It was yet another reminder to keep our endeavour in perspective.

Airport staff managed to delay our connecting flight long enough for us to clear customs and race out to the aircraft in a van. The driver eyed our team jackets and asked, "What do you guys play?"

"Mountains," I said.

Eight hours later, we arrived in Bangkok and immediately found ourselves caught up in another hassle. Kurt Fuhrich, our base camp cook, was detained at the airport because his passport had expired. Canadian embassy officials managed to secure his release after he'd spent a frustrating night stuck in the airport arrivals lounge. The rest of us had already eagerly dispersed to take in the sights.

Bangkok vividly displays some of the best and worst aspects of Asian life. Stunningly beautiful sculptures of Buddha, including the golden Wat Traimit, and intricately designed temples are located a stone's throw from large districts devoted to the sex trade. Brothels and strip joints are lined up next to VD clinics, and holiday tour operators regularly bring in planeloads of men who have purchased prostitution vacation packages. It's a bustling, noisy city, shrouded in thick smog.

After a two-day layover, we were on our way again. Our

plane made a brief stop in Calcutta, then headed north to Kathmandu. When the vast expanse of the Himalayas came into view on the horizon, we crowded eagerly around the windows for a look at the landscape. "Is that Makalu?" some climbers asked others. "Is that Manaslu? Which one's Everest?"

We were well stoked with anticipation by the time the plane touched down at Tribhuvan International Airport on the outskirts of Kathmandu. Of course, it was instant chaos from the moment the plane landed. We had 71 pieces of baggage containing personal gear and the last of the equipment. We planned to give the appearance that we were a trekking group in order to avoid paying the additional import charges usually levied on expeditions.

A few climbers had flown to Nepal in advance of the main group and had devised their own scheme to help ease our entry through customs. As a security measure, airport officials chalked a symbol on the side of each bag after slowly and methodically checking its contents. Our scouts brought their own chalk when they came to meet us and duplicated the scrawl well enough that it passed inspection at a second checkpoint. In the confusion, no one seemed to notice the subterfuge.

Amid all the hustling back and forth to our bus, and probably because of it, we suffered our first casualty. As Jim Elzinga was hauling four canvas bags out to the waiting vehicle, his right knee collapsed and he crumpled to the ground. It was the recurrence of an old injury — and in a shocking instant, it looked like one of the most determined members of the team wouldn't even get a chance at the mountain.

We were starting out with a bad luck streak, at least as far as airports were concerned. But each time an obstacle arose, Bill March and other members of the team responded quickly. Jim rushed off to get medical attention, and the rest of us made our way through the crowd of shouting taxi drivers and hotel touts to board the bus for the short drive to the Everest Sheraton.

In a city where the dead are cremated on pyres beside the Bishnumati River and the devoted worship Kumari, a living child goddess, the Everest Sheraton seemed remarkably insular, offering all the modern comforts for international travellers behind high red brick walls. Beyond those walls, the city of half a million people seemed mysterious and almost medieval. There were dark and narrow back alleys where scruffy dogs, regarded as sacred in their own right, scavenged through garbage while barefoot porters hauled heavy loads of food, wood, paper, and other trade goods on their backs. Even though Nepal is one of the poorest countries in the world, there is a spiritual wealth evident in the shrines that stand on almost every street corner in Kathmandu.

With a few days to go before our departure for the mountain, we quickly set about exploring the city on old Chinese-made bicycles. Every morning, we would spend some time sorting out piles of climbing equipment in the courtyard of Mountain Travel, our trekking agency, then ride out to Durbar Square or Swayambhunath to climb the steep steps of the "monkey temple" and take in the sights. Back at the hotel, we'd sit by the pool, sipping tea from an elegant silver service and joking about the hardships of expedition life. Jim had his leg set in a full-length cast, and it looked like he'd be out of action for months. "I'll be ready by August 20 when the climbing starts," he said, although few believed him.

It was a strange feeling to ride around Kathmandu, a city that appeared to exist in a time all its own. (It is, in fact, in a time zone of its own — 12 hours and 40 minutes ahead of Mountain Standard Time in Canada.) Garbage and sewage were dumped out in the gutters. Several streets were much too narrow for cars. In one alley, a series of open-air butcher shops were lined side by side. Slabs of yak and water buffalo meat lay out in the heat with flies buzzing around them. Some Hindu shrines nearby were covered with flowers, others with blood from animal sacrifices.

While the Sherpas of the highlands are Buddhist, Nepal is a primarily Hindu country. Just 240 kilometres wide and 800 kilometres long, it's about the same size as Florida and sits at a similar latitude. By the early 1980s, the population had reached the 15-million mark, and the country was fraught with troubling health and social issues. At that time, a Nepalese child had only a 50 percent chance of living to the age of five. Almost 90 percent of the population had unsafe drinking water. The poverty line in the country was set at $60 a year, and even at that, about 40 percent of the population lived below it. The literacy rate for men was 25 percent, for women, less than four percent. The country had 450 doctors, a ratio of one to more than 31,000 potential patients. In Canada, by comparison, the census listed one doctor for every 500 patients.

Though many of us on the expedition had studied Nepal's statistics before leaving Canada, they were nothing more to us than grim but typical Third World numbers — until we came face to face with the Nepalese people and their poverty. As we toured around Kathmandu and its surrounding areas, we saw young children cradling their infant siblings and wondered if they would be among the 50 percent who would die before they reached the age of five. We walked through village after village knowing that one area's sewage was flowing directly into the next one's drinking water. And here we were, decked out in matching Adidas tracksuits and sneakers, each of us carrying camera gear worth more than most of these people would earn in a lifetime. We felt guilty just being there, off on a quest based mainly on self-gratification, while they were in a daily struggle for survival.

Of course, foreign travellers have come to represent a major source of income for Nepal. Thousands of visitors come each year to take in the cultural attractions of Kathmandu and trek into the countryside. This means employment not only for Sherpas, but also for porters who haul loads on the trail, lodge-keepers who provide basic accommodation, and outfitters who sell an impressive array of mountaineering equipment.

Some foreign mountaineers have played a more direct role. Sir Edmund Hillary has been very active in raising money for the country where he gained fame. His Himalayan Trust has built more than two dozen schools, along with hospitals, medical clinics, bridges, and water systems for the Nepalese.

For our own part, we had already employed hundreds of porters to haul most of our food and equipment to storage sites near Everest. We had also hired close to 30 high-altitude Sherpas to work on the mountain carrying loads and climbing alongside the Canadians. They would only get a few rupees a day for the hard and dangerous work, but the pay was relatively good in terms of their national standards. Moreover, successful Sherpa mountaineers could earn fame and honours in their homeland.

It was fascinating to get a sense of Nepalese traditions, and we were gradually adjusting to the first wave of culture shock when Bill March made a stunning announcement. "We've got a serious problem," he told us. "I'm kicking Roger off the team."

According to Bill, the man who had launched the expedition and served as its first leader had seriously jeopardized the reputation of the team and its sponsors through his actions during a training climb. Roger was being dismissed for breach of the climber's contract, which included the strict morality clause. Bill would not speak publicly about the basis for his decision, but I later learned that Roger had allegedly smuggled hashish back to Canada at the end of an expedition to Annapurna by stuffing the contraband into the hollow ends of ice axes used by his team members.

Roger had flatly denied the accusation when Bill had initially confronted him months earlier. Though Bill hadn't been satisfied that Roger was telling the truth, he'd let it go at first. But when he received additional information about the allegation, Bill demanded another meeting and explanation. By this time, however, Roger had already gone to Nepal ahead of the main party. Bill suspected the headstrong climber was trying to avoid a confrontation by staying a step ahead of his accuser. He sent a message to Kathmandu ordering Roger to stay in the capital until he arrived, but Roger ignored it.

At a sombre team meeting at our hotel in Kathmandu, Bill explained his decision. Some members were surprised that Roger was being fired at such a late date. Bill explained that he'd tried to resolve the issue earlier, and that he'd wanted to meet with the man face to face again before taking decisive action. But now, with Roger already heading to the mountain, he couldn't wait any longer. The legalities of kicking Roger off the team had to be handled before we left Kathmandu. It was clear that Bill had the ammunition he needed, and the dozen climbers at the meeting voted unanimously to back his decision.

Certainly, the smuggling accusation against Roger was very serious, but it was merely one of many reasons Bill had for keeping his predecessor off the mountain. The team obviously did not have an unswerving reverence for law and order. Members made regular trips to Kathmandu's Freak Street to get the black market rate of exchange, and the sleight-of-hand technique for avoiding customs inspection at the airport was hardly exemplary conduct, either. But Roger had rashly alienated too many of the wrong people, and the climber nicknamed "Dodger" (after the shady vagabond in *Oliver Twist*) had simply become more trouble than he was worth — at least as far as Bill was concerned.

Roger was one of the strongest and most determined high-altitude climbers on the team, but he was much better in a freewheeling style of climbing where his unconventional behaviour didn't have to fit in with a pre-programmed team approach, not to mention marketing strategies and corporate images. On a more fundamental level, Bill felt he couldn't trust Roger and saw him as a threat to the team's solidarity, which was already tenuous at best.

As it turned out, no criminal charges were ever laid against Roger, and months after the climb was over, the Canadian Mount Everest Society declared that there was no concrete evidence to back up the allegation that had led to Roger's dismissal. In a carefully worded statement, however, the society also backed Bill's decision, saying he couldn't have made any other reasonable choice given the circumstances at the time.

But as our group sat together at the Everest Sheraton on July 25, 1982, such assertions were a long way off, and the climbers struggled to maintain confidence amid the serious setbacks. It looked like Jim's accident and Roger's dismissal had left us with a significantly weakened team just one week into our three-month task, and we weren't even close to the mountain yet. Later that day, we gathered in a penthouse suite at the hotel for a banquet marking our last day of luxury and the end of our easy access to Star beer. Many hoped it would also mark a change in our fortunes.

The wake-up calls came at three o'clock the following morning. Hung over, we boarded another bus for a jolting ride on the Arniko Highway, along the Sun Kosi River. Four hours later, we arrived in the small, dirty village of Lamosangu to start our trek. We knew we would be walking through monsoon rains and coping with bloodthirsty leeches in the lowlands, but the walk-in would serve as an important stage in preparing for the rigours of the mountain.

Chapter 3
The Long and Winding Trail

We began our long journey to Everest base camp by cutting across a series of steep river valleys. It meant hiking up a trail for hours, gaining 600 metres in elevation just to reach the top of a ridge, and then making a steep descent down the other side. Steve Bezruchka, who had written *A Guide to Trekking in Nepal*, calculated that the route to Everest involved a cumulative climb of close to 11,000 metres, well over the height of the mountain itself.

The overall mood of the team seemed to rise from the moment we left the end of the road at Lamosangu and began to walk under a sky that was sunny and clear despite the fact that we were still in monsoon season. "It's good to have a shakedown day," Bill said as he surveyed the first of many steep hills we had to face. Someone decided he was too chipper and slipped a heavy rock into his backpack.

There were a dozen climbers in this core group — a few had gone in earlier, and Laurie Skreslet, who was making last-minute arrangements for equipment, was to catch up later. We still didn't know if Jim Elzinga would rejoin the expedition. With a long string of Sherpas and porters hauling most of our gear, we looked like 19th-century prospectors heading out on the Chilkoot Trail. For the equivalent of $2.50, the Nepalese porters hauled loads of 27 kilograms for six hours or more. Some carried double loads for twice the pay. Meanwhile, we had the luxury of carrying light packs with just a few essentials for the trail. Team members who were used to carrying their own loads had a little trouble adjusting to the sahib mentality, but pangs of conscience quickly faded as we found it hard enough just to get ourselves up the steep hills. "The first day is always the worst," Lloyd Gallagher said as we paused for a break on a lush green ridge.

The trek to base camp was necessary for building stamina and adjusting to the air, which was losing its concentration of oxygen as we gained altitude. It was also a crucial step in developing cohesion in a team of diverse personalities. "A spirit will develop over the next few days," Gordon "Speedy" Smith had said as we'd gathered for a breakfast of porridge and tea on the first morning of the trek. "It's a good thing. The only way we're going to climb this thing is if we do it together."

The team began to loosen up as our caravan stretched out along the trail. Some members were glued to their headsets and off in their own worlds for long periods, but at other times, a few of us would break into song. "Singin' in the Rain" was a popular choice. While there were brief periods of clear skies and warm sunshine, conditions were mainly grey, and we slogged through heavy rains those first days out. We had all gone out and bought umbrellas for the trip, a mandatory piece of equipment for Himalayan trekking. Aside from protection from the rain, the inexpensive Chinese-made umbrellas offered shade when the sun became too hot. They were also good for modesty in a land where outhouses were scarce, and for fending off mangy dogs that took a dislike to foreigners.

Our expedition-issue rain gear was good to a point, but the downpour was so persistent that some of us wore garbage bags for an added layer of protection. Storms enveloped the steep valley trails with little warning. Brilliant blue skies instantly turned black and ominous. Gentle trailside streams became dangerous torrents in a matter of minutes. On the first day out, Rusty Baillie cautioned me to unhook the waistband on my backpack each time we crossed a rickety bridge. This would offer a slightly better chance of survival if I ended up in one of the swollen rivers. As we crossed a hanging bridge over the Tamba Kosi River, one of the Sherpas told us it had recently been replaced after a flash flood had hit the structure and swept 10 porters to their deaths.

We had no choice but to endure the late-summer

monsoons that blew in from the Bay of Bengal and drenched the Himalayas. The trek had to take place during the tail end of the rainy season so that we'd be at the mountain and ready to start during the brief spell of good weather in September and early October.

We were given some reprieve from the weather each night, when we could try to dry out in our tents or in local lodges or schools. On the fourth day out, we camped at Yarsa. It had been a good day's walk and we'd gotten well ahead of the porters and Sherpas. Just as we began to relax in the warm afternoon sunshine, black clouds rushed in from the southeast and blanketed our narrow valley. We were soaked within minutes and could do little more than wait for our tents to arrive. When they did, it was a hectic scene as we scrambled to get them up while digging tiny moats around them.

Even though we were preoccupied with pitching our tents, it was hard not to notice Dave Read scurrying around with nothing on but his rain jacket. "I want to keep my clothes dry," he explained. No one argued with his logic.

As we settled in and tried to get warm, Bill came around to each tent, personally delivering some hastily brewed tea and later a shot of whiskey to take off the chill. Then came the howls from one tent after another as we began to discover the leeches that had crawled into our shoes and made our socks a bloody mess. I was luckier than most: I only had two that day.

Leeches were a menace in the early days of our trek, and we tried in vain to avoid them. About two centimetres long and as skinny as a shoelace, they could get into even the tightest fitting clothes. You wouldn't feel much when the tiny beasts first took hold. It was often a case of waiting until you took off your shoes and socks and made a thorough check before you'd find them. We took special care to stay away from leaves and branches since the tenacious bloodsuckers might drop from above or crawl up from below. We were all particularly cautious while relieving ourselves along the trail. Rusty set the record for leeches one day when he lay in the grass to photograph a flower. The spot had looked safe enough, but when he got up, he counted two dozen of the creatures on his legs.

The procedure for removing them was simple. Each of us had been issued a salt shaker. It took just a little sprinkle and some quick picking. Dave Jones, one of the doctors on the team, told us that while the bites from the leeches were not harmful, we had to guard against infection since the wounds were extremely slow to heal in the wet weather.

The hardships of our trek to base camp were minor compared to the joys of meeting the warm and friendly people along the way, or to seeing the lush forests and elaborately terraced hillsides upon which farmers made use of every bit of available space. "*Namaste!*" children shouted each time we approached a small village. This meant "I salute the God in you," and we happily returned the greeting. Sacred chortens and stupas dotted the trail, and, following local custom, we kept the small shrines on our right-hand side as we passed. Prayer flags, once brightly coloured but now a faded white, waved in the wind at the tops of high passes. Religious inscriptions were carved into the rocks and sacred mani stones that lined our path. *Om mani padme om*, or "Oh hail to the jewel in the lotus," the messages proclaimed.

Still, our encounters with Nepalese culture and tradition were not always positive. On one occasion, early on in our trek, we halted for the night in Those, a tiny village near Jiri. We had just finished dinner and were preparing to settle in for the night when we heard shouts and scuffling outside the rustic lodge. Gyalgen, our *sirdar* (chief Sherpa), took Bill and Lloyd aside and explained that one of the Nepalese load carriers was claiming to have lost a rope and other pieces of climbing equipment along the trail. Gyalgen, however, suspected that the porter had stolen the equipment.

Thefts were rare among porters, and they were treated very seriously. It was a scene of rough justice as the suspected thief was brought in to our low-ceilinged dining room with his hands bound. The gear would hardly be missed from the tons of equipment on its way to the mountain, but Gyalgen said the matter had to be reported to the police in order to discourage thefts by the others. Bill and Lloyd tried to look as intimidating as possible as they demanded an explanation, and Gyalgen shouted at the frightened prisoner as he translated their questions. The frail Tamang labourer cowered. We didn't need a translator to know that he was pleading his innocence. Finally, Gyalgen said the porter would be turned over to authorities and likely face a long prison term.

The incident seemed minor at the time, but I later found out that as the porter was being taken to the police outpost for questioning, he reportedly committed suicide by throwing himself into a churning river. It was impossible to know for sure whether he had taken his own life. Jails in Nepal are grim and sentences can be very long. We were told of a custom that if a prisoner dies before his sentence is finished, a family member must serve the remaining time. Rather than place the burden on their family, accused criminals will sometimes kill themselves. There are times as well when relatives are suspected of arranging a fatal "accident" to eliminate that burden.

Though I could not have guessed the bleak outcome of the porter's arrest while we watched him being led away, I was nevertheless struck by the enormous gap between our group of privileged western adventurers and the poverty-stricken labourer. The next morning, there was little talk of the confrontation as we turned our focus to the day's route and the challenges that lay ahead.

The trekking conditions became more and more enjoyable each day as we gained elevation. The weather was improving, with bright sunny days warm enough for shorts and T-shirts. The leeches were also left behind, and we were gaining strength and enthusiasm. On the morning of August 3, we crossed a high ridge near Tragshindu and entered the magnificent valley surrounding the Dudh Kosi (Milky River). It was a significant milestone, since the river flows from the Khumbu Glacier at the base of Everest. We had begun to catch glimpses of the soaring peaks off in the distance. We were getting close to setting eyes on our goal.

Three days later, on a steep, winding trail heading up to Namche Bazaar, we gazed toward the northeastern horizon and saw the highest mountain on the earth. It was almost completely hidden behind the huge flank of Nuptse, but just the tip of the distinctive pyramid was enough to inspire awe. We rushed up the remaining switchbacks to Namche with surprising vigour, as we were now at an elevation of more than 3400 metres, the equivalent of the summits of many peaks in the Rockies.

Bill had gone up that trail a day earlier to confront Roger Marshall, who was waiting at Namche to meet up with the group. The team leader had steeled himself for the confrontation and was ready for anything, including the possibility of violence. There were times when it seemed to come close to that as the pair sat across a table from each other in a dim and dusty trekking lodge. In the course of their encounter, Roger went from denying the accusations and pleading for another chance, to threatening legal action back in Canada. He eventually backed down and admitted he'd tried to deceive Bill, saying what he thought the leader wanted to hear.

But Bill remained steadfast in his decision, and he hoped the team would see that he wasn't afraid to assert his authority while still acting judiciously. "If I'm going to make these very, very difficult personal decisions now, then on the mountain when we have equally important and dangerous decisions concerning men's lives, the team will feel those decisions have been made with as great a care and consideration as possible under the circumstances," he said as Roger prepared to head back down the trail.

Our stay in Namche marked the start of a new phase in the expedition. The turmoil surrounding Roger's dismissal was set aside at least for the time being, and the focus on Everest began to sharpen. We were out of the lowlands now and into the Khumbu region, the land of the Sherpas.

Namche Bazaar is the regional capital of the Khumbu, with government offices and police checkpoints. As the name suggests, it's also a major trading centre. After weeks of walking through villages where shops sold mainly daal bhaat (a bland lentil stew), tea, and sweet biscuits, we were happily surprised to be able to buy Swiss chocolate, granola bars, and cheese, all purchased as surplus from previous expeditions. We wouldn't catch up with our own supplies until we reached base camp, and we were starting to get tired of the food served on the trail.

There was no time to linger more than a night in Namche. We still had the final third of our three-week journey to complete. At 3500 metres, we were also getting into terrain that required us to pace ourselves and pay attention to signs of altitude sickness. It was the start of a regular routine of monitoring headaches, drinking as much liquid as possible, and trying to get a good night's sleep by hiking up to a higher altitude during the day, then returning to a lower elevation to rest.

Our caravan had gone beyond the limits of the lowland porters, and we were now sharing the trail with an impressive procession of yaks. The lumbering beasts have a certain charm but can get testy at times. We were advised to give them a wide berth and stay uphill when they passed to avoid being nudged down the steep hillsides. I also made a point of staying off the frail-looking suspension bridges while the hefty animals crossed the swaying structures.

With the mountain less than a week away, we were getting ready physically and mentally for the task ahead. The concerns of the outside world were being shed daily, and we grew accustomed to the idea that our link to that world was growing tenuous. We would eventually have a radio link to Kathmandu, but in the meantime, personal messages, as well as my stories, were carried out to Kathmandu by mail-runners who took only a few days to cover the terrain we'd spent weeks traversing. The daily hikes had succeeded in trimming a few excess pounds off most team members, and the climbers began to gain a new confidence that was occasionally carried to excess. Talk turned to speculation on how many would reach the top, not whether it could be reached at all.

Tim Auger, who had been to the Himalayas on a successful ascent of Pumori, had a cautionary word for team members who suffered an early case of summit fever. "We better get used to the fact that maybe only one or two guys are going to get to the top and the rest of us are going to spend all our time humping loads." There were assurances all around that credit would be shared, but Tim urged team members to be ready to find satisfaction in the supporting roles.

As we made our way into the mountains beyond Namche Bazaar, the team began to prepare spiritually as well. Two days out of Namche, we arrived at one of the holiest places in the Himalayas, the Thyangboche Monastery. It is a magical and exotic collection of buildings, set in a breathtakingly spectacular location. The snow-capped peaks that line the Gokyo Valley stretch out to the north. Off in the distance, Everest looms above Nuptse. Nearby, the classic beauty of Ama Dablam glistens white against the deep blue sky. The monastery itself is a magnificent white structure and exactly what you would picture in a land where there really is a place known as Shangri La. At the time of our arrival, the building was just over 50 years old (its predecessor was destroyed by an earthquake), but it had a timeless quality. It was an incredible experience to be awakened in our nearby lodge by the wailing horns of the monks and look out the window to see them gathering in their deep purple robes for a reverent sunrise procession.

It was important for us to follow the local custom and take part in an elaborate puja ceremony in the monastery. Like all major expeditions to the region in the past, we asked for a blessing from the abbot to protect us and appease hostile spirits in the mountains. The ritual is primarily for the benefit of the Sherpas, but foreigners readily take part rather than offend their climbing partners or the gods of the Himalayas.

The morning was grey and misty as we filed into the ornate inner chambers of the sanctuary while monks with lavishly plumed headgear chanted and crashed cymbals. We sat and watched as each Sherpa was presented with a syrupy liqueur and sweetmeat, along with sacred rice to scatter on the mountain. The devout Buddhists each presented a white prayer scarf to the lama, who in return placed it around the Sherpa's neck. Each was given a thin red cord with a specially placed knot in it to wear. Then it was our turn, and we gratefully accepted the blessings and well-wishes that we received in exchange for a 100-rupee donation to the monastery.

Bill had an analytical view of the significance of the blessings: "Mountaineering brings us down to a very primitive level. You either live or you die. There's an immediacy in life and death that's lacking in our modern society, and perhaps we revert to our primitive selves in terms of beliefs, and taboos, and keepsakes."

Bill had carried a good luck charm for years but had lost it in the summer of 1981 to the Nuptse rockslide. Perhaps all the good fortune it contained was used up in surviving that close call, he speculated. This time around, he would seek a sense of inner peace and solace through a special arrangement with his wife. He and Karen had pledged to think of each other daily at precisely the same time. That strong connection with his family, coupled with the blessings of the lama, were part of a way to bolster a feeling of security for the entire team, he felt. "If one projects a strong aura, this protects one's self. This aura can be reinforced by prayers, charms, and the well-wishes of family and friends. Certainly, I'm going to accept all the prayers that are offered on our behalf, whether they come from the West or the East. They can't do us any harm."

Rusty Baillie went further than anyone else in adapting Eastern spiritual traditions to the challenges of climbing. In schoolyards and campsites along the trail, Rusty performed elaborate and fluid tai chi exercises while bemused villagers looked on. "For quite a few years, I've been hearing, 'climbing's all in the head,'" he explained one evening as we sat on a high ridge above the tiny cluster of stone buildings in Pheriche. A decade earlier, Rusty had been a hot young climber, knocking off some of the hardest routes in Europe, but he soon found himself in a slump while living in Britain. "I was getting pretty scared and thought, what's going on here?"

He realized that while he was as physically able as ever, the mental side of his climbing was holding him back. So he started to look for ways to go about training his mind. He studied the relatively new field of sports psychology, but soon decided it did not apply to mountaineering. "Sports and athletics are extremely different from climbing. They're a very closed system. You have rules and regulations. You have a limited number of possible outcomes. Say you're going for a pole vault. You can give it everything you've got and you can develop a psychological strategy to just go for it completely and utterly because the worst that can happen is you just knock the pole off. With mountaineering, you can't always go for it; you can't give it everything you've got. You've got to hold something in reserve. Otherwise, you'll take a long leader fall or you'll get caught out in a storm or you've pushed too far and you're isolated and you're stranded out there. Of course, the big difference between sports and climbing is dying. The fear of getting killed is such a potent inhibitor."

Rusty began to explore different martial arts. At first he turned to aikido, but he found the movements too quick to be of use for adapting to mountaineering. Then he tried tai chi, the ancient Chinese exercises based on the movements of animals that can be performed extremely slowly or at high speed. He soon found a remarkable resemblance between climbing and his tai chi routine. "I realized I was duplicating climbing motion absolutely. It was uncanny. I'd be in the middle of a tai chi sequence and I'd think, here I am, climbing up a rock. In tai chi, you move from one balance position to another. It's the same in climbing."

He began to look at various forms of meditation to use in specific climbing circumstances. On a technical climb, he would train his mind to focus on the task at hand, while elsewhere on the mountain he would use a different approach. By altering his perspective, Rusty could heighten his overall awareness and mindfulness. He found a greater ability to see the variables — the impending storms, the clues of hidden crevasses, the dangers from avalanches, and the texture of the terrain. It was a release from traditional constraints. "You become super aware of everything that's going on. It allows you to stop doing things automatically by habit."

Rusty found that meditation was also a useful tool in

shedding extraneous mental baggage. "On an expedition, people carry a lot of mental shit around with them. They're uptight; they're worried about things. They're tense. It's a fairly normal stress response. By meditating you can regularly get rid of all that garbage so that you're not using your strength to deal with all that unnecessary stuff." Meditation allows a climber to conserve essential energy on a high-altitude endurance climb, where the challenge is frequently seen as the ability to put one foot in front of the other long enough to reach the top. It also helps clear your mind for the task at hand. "One of the great things is to learn to make a decision quickly and trust it."

While Bill and Rusty may have been more spiritually prepared than other climbers on the team, the ceremony at the Thyangboche Monastery had a deep impact on everyone — even those of us who hadn't seen the inside of a church for years. On a superficial level, it was all part of the exotic adventure, from the haunting resonance of the chants to the pungent smell of the incense. But beyond that, we could see the powerful significance of deities in the lives of the Sherpas, and as we were accepted into the realm of our Buddhist climbing partners, we wanted not only to show our respect for their beliefs, but also to share in some of the reassurances that these beliefs offered.

Chapter 4
A Sacred Place

We arrived at base camp on August 15. The advance party had done its job well, turning a patch of rubble into a reasonably comfortable tent city. Peter Spear, our consistently enthusiastic base camp manager, had gone ahead with Dave McNab and a team of Sherpas. They'd wasted no time getting to the mountain; a Spanish expedition was attempting Everest at the same time as our team, and Peter wanted first choice at a campsite.

Peter knew there was surprisingly little room on the barren valley floor, even though the area is close to one kilometre wide. Huge avalanches were breaking off the West Shoulder of Everest almost daily, and tents had to be back far enough not only to be well beyond potential slide paths, but also to withstand the powerful windblasts. Peter also had to worry about boulders that careened down from the Lho La, a high mountain pass on the Tibetan border to the north. He chose a spot on a slight rise about 500 metres from the Khumbu Icefall, the ominous maze of jumbled ice and gaping crevasses that marked the start of our route.

Jagged rocks covered the valley floor, and though it looked like we were on solid ground, our camp was actually sitting on part of the massive Khumbu Glacier. In fact, we'd spent the last day of our trek plodding 10 kilometres up the tongue of the glacier. The final approach to base camp was both exhilarating and sobering. At Dughla, one of the last settlements on the trail, we passed a row of chortens stretched out on a lonely ridge. The cairns had a ghostly look, silhouetted against wispy clouds and a wall of snow-capped mountains. "They're for the people who have died on Everest," said Dawa Dorje, a 40-year-old Sherpa and veteran of several expeditions. He explained that the ridge was not only used to erect memorials; it was also a sacred site where the men whose bodies had been recovered were cremated on pyres of rhododendron wood.

Exotic shapes surrounded us as we made our final approach. Penitentes, sharp pillars of ice, stuck up from the glacier like spearheads, poking as much as 30 metres into the air. Boulders sat on icy pedestals that looked like enormous mushrooms, the result of shade from the rocks protecting the ice underneath while the glacier melted around them. Eventually, the pedestals proved too weak and the rocks toppled over. The crashing sounds were unnerving, especially when boulders the size of Buicks fell nearby.

Disturbingly, as we neared base camp, we began to pass huge mounds of rusty cans and other refuse. After three decades of expeditions, the mountainside was sadly polluted. We were warned to carefully treat water, even at this remote location, because all the sewage from higher camps was gradually working its way down through the ice and meltwater. Peter had designated a gully for our garbage dump where our debris would eventually be incinerated.

As we walked into camp, we were amazed to see that Jim Elzinga had beaten us to the mountain and was well on his way to recovering from his knee injury. He'd had the full-length cast taken off early in Kathmandu and was now using a walking brace. To save time, not to mention wear and tear on his mending leg, he'd chartered a helicopter to fly to one of the villages near Everest, where he could begin his own acclimatization to the altitude. Since it had appeared doubtful that Jim would recover enough to do much climbing, Bill had told him he would have to pay for the $1200 flight himself. They'd agreed that if Jim proved he could still take part in the expedition, he would be reimbursed.

Even with the flight, Jim still faced a painful test of endurance. As the helicopter wound its way up the valley of the Dudh Kosi River, the pilot signalled that they would have to put down early. Heavy clouds had closed in around Namche Bazaar and he wouldn't risk flying farther into the mountains in such poor weather. Jim abruptly found himself alone at the side of the trail with a weak knee and a long climb ahead.

Hobbling slowly up to Namche, Jim came up with a plan to ride a yak the rest of the way into base camp. It seemed like a good idea at the time, but the yak had ideas of its own. Even with a Sherpa handler, the normally docile creature turned very ornery and bucked off the would-be rider. Jim persisted with caution and managed to drape himself over the animal's back. The technique worked on the flat stretches, but he still had to walk the hills.

It didn't take long for Jim to realize it would be easier on his body to walk the whole way. With a ski pole for a crutch, he made good speed and reached Pheriche from Namche in a single day, a walk of more than 12 kilometres with several steep climbs that most trekkers take two days to cover. The exertion took its toll at Pheriche, where Jim fell into the arms of Nawang, an old Sherpa friend. Jim rested at Pheriche for two nights before catching up with Peter and Dave at Lobuche for the last day's walk to base camp. "You can tell the folks back home I'm back in action," he said triumphantly when we met up with him a few days later.

Soon after our arrival, the Sherpas erected an altar in the midst of base camp, where smouldering juniper branches would be offered to the gods. Long strings of red, blue, yellow, white, and green prayer flags radiated out from the centre — each colour symbolic of the primary elements: fire, wood, earth, water, and iron. The next morning, we held a blessing ceremony to mark the start of the climb. The Sherpas made solemn offerings of rice and tsampa (roasted flour) and chanted as white smoke drifted skyward. Then we shared drinks of chang, whiskey, and rum.

Nearby, Catalan climbers from Barcelona had established base camp for their attempt of Everest's West Ridge. They had held their own prayer ceremony the same morning, and soon there was a multinational party in full swing, with songs in three different languages echoing off the mountainsides. The effect of the alcohol was heightened in the oxygen-thin air, and euphoria spread quickly. Our party stamina was short, however, and the hangovers were long. Still, we were ready the next day to begin sorting out equipment and preparing the hundreds of loads that had to be ferried up the mountain.

The plan called for establishing five high-altitude camps linked by close to eight kilometres of fixed ropes. The process of this siege-style ascent is slow and cumbersome, since climbers spend much of their time hauling loads up the mountainside to stock the higher camps. There's also a great deal of energy spent just maintaining the route. More modern techniques favour a lightweight approach, even on mountains that once took small armies to attempt. Today, alpine climbers may establish a cache of supplies up on the mountain, but for the most part, they don't depend on the backup of a large team or supply line. The smaller teams can move more quickly, and there's a better chance of each climber reaching the summit. But there isn't the same level of support if anything goes wrong.

The 1982 Canadian route broke the mountain down into distinct stages that presented specific challenges. The first, and most intimidating, was the Khumbu Icefall. This two-kilometre stretch of constantly shifting ice dominated the view from base camp and weighed heavily on the minds of the climbers who would have to search for a safe route through the tangled mess. From Camp 1, at 5975 metres, the climbing would level out for three kilometres up the Western Cwm (cwm, rhyming with room, is the Welsh word for valley). There, the main challenge would be circumventing huge crevasses while avoiding avalanches sweeping down from Everest and Nuptse. From Camp 2, at 6500 metres, the climbing would become more serious on the imposing Lhotse face at the head of the Cwm. Camp 3, at 7230 metres, would be established partway up the rock-strewn wall on a slope so steep that tent platforms had to be fitted with telescoping legs. From there, it was a gain of 700 metres up to the South Col and Camp 4. The most serious technical climbing still lay ahead on a huge spur of rock leading to the summit ridge. The challenging line held out the promise of some prestige since there was the possibility of climbing a new route on the tricky section and earning the right to call one of the most difficult features the "Canadian Spur."

Despite the ambitious plan for the upper mountain, the team still had the option of backing off the new route if it proved too difficult or dangerous and attempting the less demanding line originally climbed by Hillary and Norgay.

This decision, however, was still weeks away, and our small community prepared for a lengthy stay at base camp. Steve Bezruchka and Dave Jones set up a medical tent, organizing supplies and ensuring they were ready to provide emergency care if needed. The doctors' initial duties focused on monitoring the acclimatization of team members to the altitude of 5300 metres. They were also called on to treat an early bout of gastrointestinal illness that levelled several climbers before a reliable water purifying system was established.

After weeks of grubby living on the trail, we were eager to try the shower facilities erected on the edge of camp. Don Serl had purchased six solar heated shower bags at a West Coast marine store. Even though the air temperature was frequently close to freezing, the black plastic bags soaked up so much heat from the sun that we often had to cool the water to avoid being scalded. Dave Read enhanced the bathhouse experience by draping a pink nightie outside the showers. No one asked where he got it.

When teammates seemed to be taking the expedition or themselves too seriously, "New Wave Dave" had a way of reminding us to lighten up. "I'm on holidays," he told us constantly. He also had the best selection of tapes for the portable stereo players we'd been issued — everything from John Mayall blues to the bizarre comedy of *Monty Python's Flying Circus*. He could break into one of their routines at the drop of a straight line. "I ... I ... I never wanted to be a mountaineer; I wanted to be a lumberjack," he would tell us, then break into song.

A Sacred Place

The Canadian Everest team at Camp 1

As preparations at base camp continued, Peter Spear kept busy with his Sherpa construction crew building large stone-walled shelters for equipment storage and a combined cookhouse-dining room. Meanwhile, we kept up with the outside world via a couple of shortwave radios that offered bits of news through Radio Moscow or the British Broadcasting Corporation — the rise in tensions in the Middle East following Israel's attacks on Lebanon, the death of Princess Grace of Monaco in a car crash. Of course, the radio broadcasts offered no news from Canada. Our main link for that, at least for the first little while, was the mail brought in by Sherpa messengers. Letters from home were always eagerly read, as we began to miss the loved ones we'd left behind. One day, soon after the mail arrived, a poster of Loni Anderson appeared on the cook tent wall. The place started to remind me of an army barracks, complete with pinup jokes.

And just like in the army, there were times when the "troops" got testy over meals. Our cook, Kurt Fuhrich, had to adjust to a primitive field kitchen and modify recipes to account for the altitude. But Kurt was used to working in unusual conditions; he had cooked at an oil rig near the North Pole and served as chef to the Shah of Iran at his private casino. At base camp, he came up with some crowd pleasers when he combined stacks of Magic Pantry pre-cooked chilli, beef stew, and other main courses with local produce brought in by yaks.

We were generally appreciative as Kurt stuck to basic menus in the early days of the expedition, but he had promised treats such as high altitude pizzas, and some climbers soon grew impatient with their simple meals. "The food stinks!" Dave Read shouted as he left the cook tent one night after dinner. Kurt stormed out after Dave, threatening to punch him. They managed to sort out their differences without coming to blows, and the meals did seem to improve over the next few days.

The Nepalese government had given permission for the expedition to officially begin climbing on September 1, but we were ready to start two weeks early. We couldn't ignore the regulation, since a government liaison officer had been assigned to accompany our team. He had already complained of a breach of protocol during the trek to base camp when we'd found a refreshing swimming hole and had gone for a skinny-dip at the end of a long, hot day. "In Nepal, this is not done," he'd told Bill sternly. He was more flexible about the starting date for our climb. Since the team was ready to go early, the officer agreed to allow a "reconnaissance" of the Khumbu Icefall. For all intents and purposes, the climb had begun.

On August 18, Bill March, Dave McNab, Laurie Skreslet, and Speedy Smith began to pick their way through the icefall. The Khumbu lived up to its intimidating reputation as the climbers got a close look at the mass of broken blue ice and snow. Blocks the size of apartment buildings were wedged up against one another, and the mountaineers had to scout a route that would not only avoid collapsing seracs, but also steer clear of potential avalanches.

The Khumbu Icefall is a mountaineering nightmare, but for any team attempting Everest from the Nepalese side, it's virtually impossible to avoid. Teams that try to skirt the flank of the glacier fall prey to the avalanches and crumbling seracs that sweep down from the West Shoulder of Everest. The Catalan climbers, who were technically venturing into Tibet for their attempt of the West Ridge, had an elaborate winch to haul loads up a 300-metre rock wall to the Lho La, where they would continue on the upper stretch of the mountain.

Our team was trying to deal with the Khumbu on the mountain's own terms. By moving quickly and in the cool of the early morning darkness, when the glacier was at its quietest, we hoped to minimize the risk of being caught in the wrong place at the wrong time. The strategy seemed to work, even though there were a few reminders never to let our guard down. Bill was jolted off his feet by the windblast from one avalanche, and Speedy had a heart-stopping moment when the block of ice he was standing on dropped out from beneath his feet. The drop was just a few centimetres, but it was more than enough to show the fragile nature of the terrain.

Despite the cautious approach, a route was fixed through the icefall in just three days. "It's really excellent progress," Bill beamed. "The icefall is like a sentinel guarding access to the mountain. When you first see it, it's pretty horrifying, but like any big mountaineering problem you break it down into units."

The lead climbers had chosen a route starting up the left side of the glacier. By then we had grown accustomed to the avalanches that were regularly sweeping down Everest's West Shoulder. First there was a crack like a rifle shot, then a rolling thunder as a harmless-looking cloud of snow poured over the rocks and was swallowed up by a series of deep crevasses that protected our flank.

Speedy was construction manager for the bridges needed to span the crevasses that blocked our route. Made by patching together modified aluminum ladders and stretching a rope across as a handrail, the bridges proved to be sturdy and reliable, and we began talking about the "Trans-Canada Highway" that snaked through ice and snow to Camp 1.

Even with the route in place, climbers and Sherpas were assigned to constantly maintain it. Heavy snowfall buried long sections of the yellow nylon rope that we used to clip onto and protect ourselves from a fall. The "road crew" also had the unnerving task of reinstalling bridges damaged by the shifting ice. At times, spans were left dangling on their anchor lines when crevasses opened wider. There were also times when the metal was bent and twisted as walls of ice were pushed together with unimaginable force.

The entire team of Sherpas and sahibs, as we called ourselves, was divided into groups to haul 450 loads of food, equipment, oxygen bottles, and other gear up to Camp 1. At 30 loads a day, it would take at least two weeks, not counting days lost to bad weather. While I was on the expedition to provide coverage for Southam News, Bill expected me to help with the load-carrying since I would be using supplies the same as anyone else on the upper part of the mountain.

The workdays were exhausting. On the mornings when I was scheduled to do a carry, the alarm on my watch would go off at 2:30 and I'd start to shuffle around in the dark, trying to pull on socks and long underwear while still in the warmth of my double-layered sleeping bag. I eventually had to get out to add a layer of Helly Hansen for insulation and a Sun Ice suit for protection from the wind. I would then pull on my plastic-shelled double boots and gaiters, grab my climbing gear, and head down to the cook shelter. When the weather was clear, I'd pause to gaze at the night sky, with stars shining brilliantly

73

through the thin air. It was hard to work up much of an appetite at that hour, but I would try to drink as much tea or coffee as I could, and at least have a bowl of granola or oatmeal. After breakfast, we'd pack water bottles, trail mix, and chocolate bars for later, then pick up our loads for the day.

Setting out from camp, we looked like hard-rock miners with our headlamps lighting up the path just a few paces ahead. Off in the distance, the climbers assigned to check and repair the route from overnight damage appeared as tiny dots zigzagging up through the icefall. We had to cross half a kilometre of rocky moraine to reach the start of the fixed rope, where we clipped a sling from our safety harnesses onto the polypropylene line.

The bridge over the first crevasse was guaranteed to eliminate any lingering drowsiness. The adrenalin started to pump just at the thought of edging across the deep chasm, which looked particularly foreboding in the moonlight. The standard crossing technique required balancing on the slippery rungs of the ladders with steel crampons that were not made for walking on aluminum. The Sherpas had no qualms about getting down on their hands and knees if they felt uneasy about a tricky span, and a few of us didn't hesitate to follow suit. In most cases, however, it was easier just to walk slowly with a tight grip on the handrail and a strong faith in our bridge-builders.

The Sherpas gave clear indication about the degree of danger they sensed as we moved through the darkness. On moderate stretches we could hear them slowly repeating their mantra — *Om mani padme om* — over and over again. On steep terrain, or when an avalanche broke loose in the distance, they quickened the pace of their prayers. When they started to sound like a phonograph record on high-speed, we knew it was time to worry.

Team members soon became familiar with the route through the icefall and named landmarks along the way. The traverse was a long, snow-filled gully bordered by immense blocks of ice. "They're like sugar cubes except they're fifty [15 m] or sixty feet [18 m] across each side," Speedy said after seeing them for the first time. Above the traverse, the terrain seemed less exposed to falling ice and became known as "the meadow" or "the valley." An enormous wedge farther up was dubbed "the Canmore Hotel," in honour of a favourite drinking spot back home. The route then scaled a series of cliffs to a short flat stretch filled with smaller blocks that became known as "the graveyard." We called an overhanging wall of ice near the top of the icefall "the ship's prow." No one lingered in its shadow. The fundamental rule was to move quickly through areas of obvious danger and rest in safe spots.

Despite the danger, the Khumbu had an awesome beauty, and each journey was an unforgettable experience. At times it was like walking through an ice palace, replete with pristine white corridors, crystal staircases, and lofty frozen turrets. On straightforward terrain, it was easy to settle into a slow plodding rhythm and forget for a moment where you were. Then you'd turn a corner and be startled by the magnificent view of Pumori off in the distance, changing from a soft pink to a brilliant gold as it caught the early morning sun.

The most stirring view was saved for last. On my first climb through the icefall, after climbing for hours, watching and listening for hazards and trying to ward off headaches and fatigue, I scaled a final 10-metre wall of ice. When I pulled myself over the top, the vast expanse of the Western Cwm spread out before me. I was dazzled by the intense sunlight sparkling off the hoar frost. The West Shoulder of Everest rose 1000 metres above us on the left. The ridge of Nuptse was an equally high wall of snow and ice on our right. In between, the valley floor was stark white, and, unlike the tangled mess of the icefall, it seemed to rise gently before coming to an abrupt end at the foot of Lhotse.

"The Western Cwm is almost a sacred place for climbers, the cwm of silence," Bill had said to me earlier. But there was little time to savour the view or dwell on the history surrounding the valley. I dropped my load of ropes and climbing hardware at the growing cache of supplies and began to head back down before the sun became too intense. Even though we started out bundled against the sub-zero cold, by midmorning we could strip down to T-shirts for the return trip, when temperatures rose to 35 degrees Celsius.

Experienced climbers could reach Camp 1 from base camp in just three hours, but as a novice, it took me almost twice as long. I had to hurry to avoid being caught out in the afternoon sun, not only to escape the heat, but also to get out of the icefall before the risk of avalanches and serac collapse became too high. "This is a hell of a place to be learning about glacier travel," Don Serl told me one morning as we both sat leaning against a serac in the midst of a carry.

Within a few days, the expedition had ferried 130 loads through to Camp 1 and an advance team had scouted a location for Camp 2. On one carry, I had to give up halfway through the icefall when my head began to throb and my stomach started to churn. The early signs of altitude sickness were unmistakable, and I knew the remedy was straightforward — go back to lower altitude and rest. Dave Jones suggested I stay in base camp for a couple of days.

Life in base camp was settling into a routine, with Canadians and Sherpas sharing a schedule of alternating rest days and carries. But the warm midday sun was causing a few problems in the camp. A boulder the size of a truck toppled over when its icy platform collapsed in the heat. The rock landed on the edge of a tiny rivulet where two Catalans had been washing clothes the day before. With yet another hazard to worry about, Peter initiated regular patrols. Whenever a rock near base camp looked like it was just about ready to roll, he enlisted a crew of Sherpas to nudge the boulder into a safer spot. It was all part of life on the glacier, where the imperceptible flow of the steadily melting ice required constant repairs to our makeshift shelters. Our semi-enclosed outhouse needed special attention, and even with several design improvements, visits tended to be adventures in themselves due to the improvised seat perched above a deep drop. A securely anchored safety line was installed to prevent accidents.

On August 26, a four-man team led by New Zealander Peter Hillary (son of Sir Edmund) set up camp near ours to prepare for an ambitious attempt of Lhotse. The group had already arranged to take advantage of the Canadian passageway through the icefall before veering off in the Western Cwm to scale Everest's sister peak. Along with the shared route, the Lhotse team had another connection to the Canadian team. Adrian Burgess, Alan's twin brother, was on Hillary's expedition, and the siblings had a family reunion at base camp.

August 26 had been extremely productive for us, with 42 loads carried through to Camp 1. Nevertheless, climbers were starting to get edgy about repeated exposure to the dangers of the icefall. John Amatt had heard a serac collapse just behind him as he'd made his descent that day. And Speedy had slipped while crossing a flake of ice, sliding for a couple of metres before his fall was halted by a fixed rope.

The idea of repeated trips through the most dangerous section of the Khumbu went against the grain of the climbers, and Bill could see the strain building.

"How many times do I have to go through?" climbers began to ask.

Bill had a stock answer: "As many times as it takes to get all the supplies and gear up to climb the mountain."

Chapter 5
Heroic Hearts

Buoyed by the solid early progress, climbers were ready for another good day's work on August 27. Rusty and a group of Sherpas set out early, but the snowfall was heavy and they took longer than usual to open up the route. Tim Auger was getting ready to head up the mountain when he sensed an uneasiness among the Sherpas. He quickly conferred with Al Burgess and Lloyd Gallagher. The trio knew very well that the veteran Himalayan mountaineers were acutely aware of potential dangers. They decided to abort the carry, and Lloyd rushed outside to call the lead team back.

Later that morning, we met to establish a procedure for evaluating the risk each day and calling off carries if needed.

The climbers agreed that heavy snowfall at base camp would mean automatic cancellation, and that a Canadian would be in the advance party equipped with a radio to relay conditions back to base or to receive a message to turn back if necessary. With a light snowfall on August 28, 20 Sherpas and 14 climbers made their way through the icefall, hauling loads, re-breaking trail, and repairing bridges.

A day later, the expedition was poised to reach an early milestone, with Bill March, Tim Auger, Al Burgess, Dave McNab, and a team of Sherpas set to occupy Camp 1. It was the first night that climbers would be staying above base camp. From Camp 1, they would be able to scout out a route to Camp 2 farther up the Western Cwm and relay weather conditions and other observations back to base in an attempt to keep closer watch on the avalanche danger.

The advance team soon settled on a spot for Camp 2, while we continued to carry loads to the Camp 1 depot. That evening at base camp, we finished dinner with cake and songs for Don Serl's birthday. We had a late-night radio check with the climbers at Camp 1, and Bill said he would call down at 5 a.m. to relay weather information. The team had talked about the possibility of an earlier call, but conditions seemed good, and after a long day's work at high altitude, Bill was reluctant to get up at 3 a.m. or have anyone else handle the chore.

When we awoke just after 2 a.m. on August 31, the sky was overcast but there was little new snow in base camp. It looked like we would have another good day on the mountain.

Pat Morrow and Rusty Baillie set out early with Sherpa guides Ang Rita and Ang Dawa to clear the route and make necessary repairs to the fixed line and bridges. Blair Griffiths, Peter Spear, and I followed behind with a larger contingent of Sherpas. As usual, we spread out into a long formation, with the Sherpas anxious to move on ahead and get in and out of the icefall as quickly as possible.

The lead climbers began to slog through fresh snowfall soon after they started up the fixed rope, but they expected that cooler conditions up above would mean a light and less dangerous powder that wouldn't become hazardous until late in the day. Rusty stopped to fix a ladder with Ang Rita, while Pat and Ang Dawa went ahead to break trail. Blair soon passed the work crew and joined Pat in the lead, and Peter caught up to Rusty just after 5 a.m. I was taking it slow and easy, remembering my bout of altitude sickness the last time out. The sky was turning a pale grey in the pre-dawn light just as I was getting ready to climb up and start across the traverse. I stopped for a moment to take off my headlamp.

Up in Camp 1, the advance team was waking to find that a heavy snowfall had blanketed their tents. Bill radioed down to the climbers leading the carry, but we were well into the icefall and spread out along the route. I had become so accustomed to avalanches crashing off in the distance that, at first, I paid little attention to the crack of thunder high up on the West Shoulder of Everest. It was almost routine to hear the sharp blast signalling the start of the slide and the low rumble that slowly faded as the tumbling snow and ice fell into crevasses far off to our left.

But this avalanche was different. The roar kept getting louder and louder. At first, there was a rush of cold air, then the hiss of snow blowing against the seracs beside me. In an instant, a cloud of white powder blasted over the ridge just above me. I scrambled behind a block of ice, crouched down, and pulled my pack over my head, hoping it would create an airspace that could be a lifesaver if I was buried. There was no time for fear, but I knew that if it was a slide as big as many we'd seen, it wouldn't make much difference what I did. In a few seconds, it was all over. I'd merely been dusted by a few centimetres of snow. Surprisingly, I wasn't shaken up at the time by the close call. That would come later, when I stopped to think about what could have come over that ridge.

An eerie silence descended on the icefall as I stood up and shook the fine-grained snow off my back. Then I heard faint shouts from above and realized how lucky I had been. The main avalanche had swept across the route just ahead. Its devastating force and speed had created the windblast that not only covered me with loose snow, but also shook tents in Camp 1 and down at base camp. A fracture line had opened up high on Everest's West Shoulder, and a two-kilometre-wide avalanche had cascaded toward us. Crevasses swallowed some of the slide, but much of it was airborne, and it split into long fingers that reached deep into the icefall.

Blair, Pat, and several Sherpas were 300 metres farther up the route when they were hit.

Pat had zero visibility and little warning when the wall of snow and ice came crashing down on him. Blair could faintly see the billowing mass of white out of the corner of his eye and tried to warn Pat, but there was no time. Pat dove behind a serac, and he could feel Blair's weight just beyond him on the rope. But there was no way that Pat could pull him to safety. It was all Pat could do to struggle back behind the serac each time the rope dragged him toward the slide path. He couldn't hear anything from Blair.

Peter and Rusty had been just behind Pat and Blair but had stopped to work on an unstable bridge. Four Sherpas hadn't wanted to wait for the repairs and had rushed across the crevasse while the sahibs had held the ladder steady. Minutes before the avalanche hit, Peter tried to radio Lloyd and ask him to send up more bridge sections, but he was having trouble transmitting. A fresh set of batteries had failed and he was getting frustrated with the equipment. He noticed the letters "UL" on the side of his radio. "What does UL mean, out of luck?" he joked to Rusty. Then he heard the slide, getting louder and louder like an approaching freight train. It was only 50 metres away when he saw the churning snow coming straight toward them.

"Avalanche!" he screamed at Rusty, and within seconds he was being whipped back and forth on the fixed line. He tried desperately to keep his arms and legs spread out and kick with his feet to stay on top of the flowing mass. Rusty, meanwhile, barely had time to curl into a ball before he was hurled 25 metres down the mountainside and left buried up to his chest. Slowly, he managed to dig himself out of the snow that was setting like concrete. He saw Peter's boot sticking out of the snow above him and raced over with Ang Rita to free him. Peter had managed to keep an airspace clear around his face, but he was in severe pain, his body twisted and contorted around the taut fixed line. Ang Rita relieved some of the pressure by cutting the rope.

In a frantic exchange of radio calls, the Canadians and Sherpas were all accounted for — except for three Sherpas who had been caught in the middle of the traverse. The advance party began a quick search, with climbers and Sherpas moving in from base camp and Camp 1 to aid in the rescue attempt. They started to probe the hard-packed snow with long poles and dig a trench to uncover the fixed rope.

It was close to an hour before members of the team spotted a hand buried just beneath the surface, and they raced to carve away the solid mass that entombed Pasang Sona. His body was cold and lifeless, but the climbers put him in a sleeping bag and Rusty crawled in to give him some warmth. Steve spent 30 minutes attempting cardiopulmonary resuscitation, even though he knew there was faint hope for the 40-year-old Sherpa. "If it were me, I'd want someone to at least try," Steve thought as he kneeled over the body and struggled again and again to revive the lifeless figure.

The search for the others continued until 9 a.m., but it was grimly apparent that after almost four hours under the snow, they had no chance of survival. Moreover, the rescuers were in danger of being caught in a second slide. The final roll call confirmed that Dawa Dorje, 40, and Ang Tsultim, 20, were the two still buried. There would be no further attempts to recover their bodies.

The loss of Dawa Dorje was particularly hard on the team. He had been on Annapurna IV with Don, Roger, and Alan. And Pat and I had spent a fascinating afternoon with him during the final approach to base camp. He'd guided us to Pangboche to see the region's oldest monastery. According to local lore, part of the scalp from a yeti is kept within its walls. We didn't get a chance to see the relic, but Dawa had led us to an inner room lined with prayer scrolls and covered with brilliant Buddhist images. He'd later reassured us that we hadn't missed much by not seeing the dried-out patch of skin with tufts of fur — many people believe the scalp really came from a goat or bear.

As team members and Sherpas brought down Pasang's body, the reality of the tragedy sank in. For some climbers, it was their first encounter with death in the mountains. Even for veterans like Alan Burgess, the loss was hard to accept, especially since the victims were Sherpas. Bill had assigned Al to stay up at Camp 1 during the rescue attempt in order to take care of Sungdare, a Sherpa who was suffering from snow blindness. Al recorded his thoughts on tape in the wake of the disaster. He couldn't understand why the carry hadn't been aborted. He had just woken up at Camp 1 when the avalanche broke. "It kept on roaring and roaring and roaring. I thought ... this is a big one ... I don't know why they set off this morning. We're responsible for the Sherpas. They're working for us. When we ask them to do a job, we should be confident in our judgment that job is possible and safe. They'll follow you into bloody hell if you asked them to and we have no right to ask them to do that. We have no right to ask them to walk into avalanches."

Pasang's body was wrapped in a sheet and placed in a rocky enclosure at base camp, with a light burning nearby. Soon after, Sherpas began to burn more juniper at their altar. As I watched them fan the flame, I noticed three ravens perched on a ledge beside the shrine. A fourth jet-black scavenger joined them, a symbol of another tragedy to come.

It was September 1, the official start of the post-monsoon climbing season, and the Canadian expedition was already starting to fall apart. Don Serl was ready to leave the mountain, and others were on the verge of following. That morning, Steve, John, and Bill left camp early to accompany the Sherpas as they carried Pasang's body down to Lobuche and on to Dughla, where he would be cremated on that high mountain ridge. Word had already been sent down the valley to the families of the dead. Bill would meet with them, pay a small insurance settlement, and try to offer some comfort.

The impact of the accident was painfully underscored

as Pasang Sona's wife and daughter arrived in Lobuche, followed by Ang Tsultim's father, and finally Dawa Dorje's pregnant wife. A lama arrived to prepare the body and guide Pasang's spirit into the next life. Porters had been summoned from the lowlands to bring loads of rhododendron wood for the funeral pyre.

In base camp, team members spent the day quietly wondering whether the mountain could be climbed safely and if it still made sense to continue. I made a personal decision not to go through the icefall again. I had hoped to get to the high altitude camps and relay stories back from there, but the avalanche had shown just how dangerous and unpredictable the mountain could be. Dave Read, Blair Griffiths, and I sat in Dave's tent talking about the climb. Both Dave and Blair were determined to continue. I hadn't gotten to know Blair very well during the expedition. The 33 year old had climbed in Peru and Alaska as well as the Coast Range in British Columbia, and he was along to do the same job that I was there to do — document the climb for Canadians back home. Blair had ambitions of going as high as possible on Everest, and he had given a great deal of thought to the dangers ahead. After the ceremony at Thyangboche, he had written in his journal, "I don't want to die, but if the pale horse should decide to come along, there isn't a better cathedral to stay in."

Later that day, while some climbers were still thinking about going home, the rest of the team decided to return to the icefall, repair the bridges damaged by the slide, restore the fixed line, and press on. Early the next morning, Blair, Dave Read, Rusty, and two Sherpas formed a work crew to repair the damaged bridges, while five other sahibs and ten Sherpas hauled loads up to Camp 1. The New Zealand team was set to make its first carry through the icefall as well. It had been a beautiful clear night, and our team seemed ready to make a fresh start.

It was about 9:15 a.m. when the shouting started. One of the New Zealand climbers watched in horror as a massive section of the traverse collapsed, sending huge seracs tumbling. From a distance, it was difficult to see if anyone was in the area, but we quickly formed a rescue party.

Dave Jones filled my pack with emergency medical equipment. I grabbed a radio and set out for the icefall. The radio transmissions that morning relayed the grim news.

Rusty Baillie: "There's been a terrible accident in the traverse. I think Blair is dead and maybe also Dave Read and a Sherpa."

Dave McNab: "Base camp this is Dave. Do you read? Over."

Peter Spear: "Go ahead, Dave."

Dave: "Okay, Peter. What we've got is we've passed Sungdare, and right now we're standing with Nawang and four other Sherpas."

Peter: "Are they on their way down and are they okay?"

Dave: "That's affirmative. Nawang says Dwayne, James, Jim, Laurie, and Lloyd are all above the traverse, and he believes that they are safe."

Peter: "Ten-four on that. Who are the suspected people in the traverse?"

Dave: "We suspect Rusty Baillie, Dave Read, and Blair Griffiths."

Peter: "Yes, Rusty has talked to us so we know he is okay. They're doing some excavating but we've not heard any more word than that."

Dave: "We understand that Dave Read is also okay. We're not sure as to the condition of Blair Griffiths."

Don Serl (a few minutes later): "I've just talked to four Sherpas on the way down. Two of them apparently are the two Sherpas who were in the traverse when it collapsed. They say that they are okay but apparently a sahib has been crushed by ice in the chest and apparently is dead. I don't know who it is but the suspicion would be that it may be Blair."

Alan Burgess: "There's Dave Read and Rusty Baillie here.

Everyone is more or less out of it except Blair, affirmative, 100 percent dead. His head and shoulders are out and he was crushed. Over."

Peter: "Repeat please."

Alan: "Al here to base. Speaking here ... standing here speaking to Rusty and Dave Read. They're both okay. Blair Griffiths is dead. He's stuck between two ice blocks and his head and shoulders are above. We must now decide if we're going to get the body. There's a possibility the blocks may move if we remove him, Rusty says, but I'm prepared to go up and try anyway, at least to have a look at the situation. Over."

Rusty: "Peter, are you reading me? Over."

Peter: "Go ahead, Rusty."

Rusty: "Pretty calm here. My recommendation is that no climbers go anywhere near the traverse and that Blair's body is left. Repeat. I think that we should definitely not undertake any recovery of Blair's body. No climbers should go anywhere near the traverse. Over."

Peter: "My decision coming from base camp would be that given the fact that it's been ascertained that Blair is dead, at this time I feel ... We should come back for the safety of the people ... the rescue party that is on the mountain should come back immediately."

A small group of Sherpas arrived back in camp first. Then the main rescue party returned. Climbers who were full of confidence and optimism just three days earlier were dazed and shaken. How could things have gone so wrong? How could the mountain wreak such havoc in so little time? If climbing was a game of odds, how could one team be so unlucky?

Slowly, we congregated in the cook tent to try to make some sense of the latest accident and plan what to do next. Rusty was deeply affected by the two accidents. He had come close to death both times, and his eyes revealed a deep sadness, yet he recounted the events of the icefall collapse with remarkable composure. He knew he wasn't going back on the mountain again.

Rusty had stopped to work on a shaky ladder with Dave Read, Blair, and two Sherpas — Nima Tsering and Pasang Tenzing. Dave and Nima were on one side of the bridge. Rusty, Blair, and Pasang were on the other. Rusty was sorting out ropes. The sky was a clear and brilliant blue.

"There were these big explosions and everyone just looked up," Rusty recalled for the group. "Then [the icefall] started moving. I was walking around on my crampons and trying to keep flat. Then my block [of ice] would tilt up and I'd try to run up to the top. Then it would go flat. And when it started to go, I thought, 'Okay, this is it. I want to go really calmly. I don't want to panic or anything like that.' And then it was flat and I started looking around. Then the second lot started coming down. All the big seracs started coming down and I had to go to the end of my block and this serac came down about 10 feet [3 m] away from me. I thought the second one was going to get me. I thought, 'Well I can either jump into the crevasse or I can wait and see if it misses me.' And it missed me and I was left standing there."

He took a moment to absorb the scene of utter desolation, then made a grim discovery.

"I looked out and there was Blair … obviously dead … crushed. And then I looked down in this hole and way down, 20 [6 m] or 30 feet [9 m] down, was Dave with a Sherpa on top of him."

Dave's account of the disaster was equally chilling. The "road-mending" crew had just decided that a temporary patch job on the bridge was secure enough to leave for at least a few days. As they were preparing to move on, a Sherpa arrived with a 2.5-metre-long ladder, and the crew figured they might as well stay and add it to the other two sections. The sun had just come around from behind the West Flank of Everest, and Dave had crossed to the lower end of the bridge to get some snow goggles. Blair, meanwhile, was pounding on one section with a hammer until it finally slid into place. Dave looked up toward Blair, who had stopped to survey their work.

"Then the whole glacier started to shudder, shake, shimmy and move similar to the streets of San Francisco prior to an earthquake," Dave told us. "At first I thought there must be an avalanche somewhere, and then I realized it wasn't an avalanche. It was the glacier moving.

"At that particular instant, the bottom dropped out of my world. What we were standing on slid into the crevasse and all I can remember is I was sliding down through large blocks, big blocks around my head as I was passing them and they were going over the top of me and I thought, 'This is it.' This must have lasted for 10 to 15 seconds, which seemed like an eternity."

As suddenly as it began, the horrific tumbling of the massive blocks ended. Dave was wedged between two big ice blocks that trapped his legs. Over his head, two other blocks were leaning against one another, providing a life-saving airspace. He quickly realized he wasn't alone when he lifted a hat lying nearby and discovered there was a Sherpa buried beneath it. He scraped the snow from the man's face just as Rusty poked his head around a block of ice and shouted, "My God, you're alive."

"Yes, of course I'm alive, but can you stop this Sherpa from struggling?" Dave replied.

After calming down the Sherpa, Rusty lowered a roped and pulled him to safety. Dave was still trapped, but he managed to dig one leg out of the snow. He then began hacking at the tangle of ropes wrapped around his other leg. After almost 15 minutes, he was able to free himself. Then he asked about Blair's condition.

"Sorry, mate, but he's dead," Rusty said.

Dave was struck by how peaceful Blair looked trapped between two huge blocks of ice. After confirming beyond doubt that Blair had died, Dave shook Blair's hand and said how sorry he was.

It was a shattering day for the team members at base camp. It was far worse for Bill. He'd spent the night before consoling relatives of the deceased Sherpas, making arrangements for Pasang's cremation, and trying to put the accident that had killed the Sherpas into perspective. With the mantle of leadership came the responsibility for those Sherpas' lives. He watched in deep sorrow as the lama prepared Pasang's body and lit the flames that would eventually turn it to ashes.

Bill and Steve were getting ready to trek back up to base camp when a Sherpa mail-runner handed them a note from Peter Spear: "Bill, Very bad news. We had a major collapse in the icefall this morning ... and Blair Griffiths was killed. Rusty Baillie and Dave Read were near him at work on a bridge when it happened and they had close calls, but were unhurt. Blair, however, is dead. I'm very sorry. Please give us a radio call when you're free. — Peter."

The tragedy had shaken all of us, but Bill reacted with unexpected calm. He had already shut down his emotions as a way of coping with a very dangerous mountain. There would be time to grieve later. As long as we remained on Everest, the only way Bill could continue to lead was to take a cold and hard approach — to reduce decisions to the fundamental principles of mountaineering. It had become a matter of survival, but it was a philosophy that put him in conflict with most of his team.

When Bill radioed base camp and learned that volunteers were preparing to recover Blair's body the following day, he flatly ordered the team to leave Blair in the icefall. He didn't want to risk any more lives. There was no possibility of returning the body to Canada because of the time and distance involved, and Bill, who had just witnessed a cremation, knew that the emotionally charged ceremony could push more climbers toward quitting the expedition. There was also the practical consideration of whether there was enough wood available nearby for the funeral pyre.

Over the weeks that had passed, Bill had exercised an autocratic form of leadership on the mountain. He consulted with the team about various aspects of the ascent, but there were no votes taken on his decisions. This time, however, the climbers weren't willing to accept his ruling. There are many bodies buried in the snow and ice on Everest, but it seemed too heartless to lower Blair into a crevasse and leave him behind. In repeated radio calls, Peter stressed how strongly the climbers felt about recovering Blair's body. Bill finally relented, knowing that some team members were ready to leave the expedition no matter what he decided.

Early the next morning, Don Serl, Al Burgess, Tim Auger, and Dave McNab set out from base camp to bring Blair down. Climbers stationed at Camp 1 began to descend around the same time in order to replace the fixed line that had been torn apart in the avalanche and icefall collapse. Laurie slipped and fell while working on one of the twisted bridges, smashing his ribs against a block of ice. Tim, meanwhile, hacked away at the ice around Blair, and the climbers quickly bundled Blair up for his final trip down from the mountain. It was hard and awkward work. The climbers were tense as they moved as quickly as possible, bringing the body back down through the terrain that had proved so deadly.

At base camp, we placed Blair on a stretcher equipped with a single wheel (to assist in long evacuations). Even with the device, it was an exhausting day as we carried our teammate over the rugged glacier and down to Lobuche. In a way, it felt somehow rewarding to get Blair off the mountain, away from the barren and seemingly malevolent terrain and back to a landscape dotted with trees, wildflowers, and grassy slopes. The following morning was cold, cloudy, and misty as we walked down the valley to that lonely, windswept ridge lined with chortens.

The funeral service was brief but very moving. Bill led us in the Lord's Prayer, then each of us said a few words in Blair's honour. Tim had written a poem and read it slowly and quietly as we stood beside the high pile of branches cradling the makeshift shroud:

This is the way of all eternity.
As we see him now, so shall we be.

Heroic Hearts

When the time comes to follow him
to where the mountain wind blows,
go as he does, with a good heart.

I saluted Blair as a journalist who was willing to risk his life to cover a story. Then, just before the branches were lit, Dave McNab placed a few wildflowers on the shroud. I opened a well-worn paperback of poetry that Blair had brought along and read the final lines from Tennyson's *Ulysses*:

Tho' much is taken, much abides; and tho'
We are not now that strength which in old days
Moved earth and heaven; that which we are, we are;
One equal temper of heroic hearts,
Made weak by time and fate, but strong in will
To strive, to seek, to find, and not to yield.

Chapter 6
A New Beginning

As we made the long, mournful walk back to camp, we were alone with our thoughts. It was staggering to consider that we'd been on the mountain for less than three weeks and the expedition was on the brink of collapse. The "Big Red Machine" had been stopped in its tracks. The confidence and exuberance that was so pervasive a week earlier was completely gone. The expedition was humbled, and each climber now had to decide whether to stay or go.

For some, the decision came easily. Don Serl had already made up his mind after the Sherpas died. The death of Blair, his closest friend on the mountain, only served to deepen his sorrow and resolve. "Blair, my friend, we've shared a few goals together and I was really looking forward to sharing this one with you. I'll go back to my home hills and I guess you'll go off to some home of your own," he had said at the funeral.

The fatalities had cast a pall over the expedition, and Don could see no justification for continuing. A phrase kept returning to him. It was from Walter Bonatti, a revered Italian climber: "No mountain is worth so much as one death."

Rusty Baillie had also considered pulling out after his first brush with death in the avalanche, but had decided to stick it out. "For some reason that I'll never understand, I just thought, 'Well, I'll give it one more go.' Theoretically, everything I came up with said I should go, but my gut feeling said 'stay.'"

His second close call, however, was enough to change his mind. Rusty believed there was a way to calculate the odds and come up with a plan to minimize the risks on Everest, but he came to see the Khumbu as a deadly enigma. Over a cup of strong tea at base camp, he told me how he had come to his decision. "I thought there was a way to make it more predictable, but this route is dangerous to begin with and one of my concessions to being married is that I'm not going to do routes like this anymore. I'm not sure it's the kind of mountaineering I'm into where it's more a matter of luck than your climbing skills. That's not what mountaineering means to me. It's not what the game's all about."

Bill March was determined to stay, but he was equally adamant that he wouldn't try to talk others into it. He couldn't guarantee there wouldn't be another accident, and if he persuaded the climbers to stay, the weight of responsibility would be intolerable. Climbers could take some time to wrestle with their consciences if they were uncertain, but Bill took a hard line with members who decided to leave. He wanted them out of camp as soon as possible. The longer they stayed, he thought, the more likely others would join them. He had little patience with climbers who expressed doubts about his hard-nosed approach.

Jim Elzinga was among these doubters. Despite enduring pain and hardship to rejoin the team after his knee injury, Jim questioned whether the climb should continue, whether it could possibly be done with a reasonable level of safety, and whether the potential for success was worth the risk. He and Bill had a heated argument in Lobuche. Neither saw room to compromise.

Later, Bill took Tim Auger aside and quietly told him that it was understandable if Tim wanted to leave. Tim had a wife and child back home, just as Bill did, and he needed to consider them. Tim felt he was being invited to leave, that Bill had incorrectly singled him out as the main instigator of the team's decision to recover Blair's body. Bill felt that the recovery had been a high-risk gesture, based on sentiment and compassion, and Tim got the clear message that there was little room for those humanitarian factors on this expedition.

"Climbing Everest is not a kid's game. Climbing Everest is extremely dangerous and a very hard game," Bill told Steve Bezruchka as they sat in a trailside lodge called The Promised

Land, nursing beers and trying to sort out conflicting responses to the accidents. "Unless you have your shit together and you know what you are doing, you shouldn't be there."

For many of the young climbers, personal commitment to the expedition was not the issue. Four men had been killed in the icefall, and no one could say for certain whether it was because of bad weather, bad judgment, or bad luck. There was an ethical question whether it was possible to claim success on a climb where lives were lost, but the deaths raised another fundamental doubt among the climbers as well. Was it possible to go back into the icefall and know that their skills and experience would be enough to give them a fighting chance?

For some, it was obvious that the odds were stacked against them on that route, during that season, with that team. Tim Auger and Dave McNab pulled out of camp late in the afternoon of September 5. Jim Elzinga, James Blench, Rusty Baillie, and Don Serl left the following morning. Dave Jones, who had been having difficulty adjusting to the altitude, decided to pack it in as well, since he could travel with the departing climbers and count on their assistance if he had trouble on the walk out.

As the dissenters headed down the trail, the tension that had been straining base camp since the accidents gradually began to ease. The anger toward Bill was barely concealed from some who packed their gear to begin the long journey home. Many who stayed had little sympathy for the point of view of those who were leaving.

It was tempting to view the division along nationalist lines. The group that left consisted mainly of the younger Canadian-born mountaineers. The older British-born climbers — Bill March, Al Burgess, Dave Read, and Gordon Smith — made up the core of those determined to stay. New Zealander Lloyd Gallagher, who was a loyal ally of Bill's, continued to back the leader as well.

On the surface, it looked like the foreign-born climbers were the ones most prepared to follow Bill's hard line and persevere for the honour of their adopted country. It was easy to speculate that the more experienced climbers had stayed on because they'd had more exposure to death in the mountains and were better equipped to deal with the tragedies. But in truth, there was no simple explanation. In his rescue work for the national parks, Tim Auger had seen more tragedies than anyone else on the team, and no one had endured a more personal loss than Jim Elzinga, who had recovered John Lauchlan's body in the Rockies.

Though most of the Canadian-born climbers chose to leave, three decided to stay — Dwayne Congdon, Laurie Skreslet, and Pat Morrow. Dwayne, 26 years old and the youngest climber on the team, had initially been determined to leave with his close friends and long-time climbing partners. He even packed his gear and sent it off to Kathmandu, but he wanted to remain in base camp briefly in order to wait for his girlfriend, Colleen Campbell, who was trekking into the mountain. The stay gave him a chance to reflect on the conflicting rationales. "It's impossible to justify the deaths or put everything in its proper moral position. You can't do that. I can't do that if I stay, and I can't do that if I go," he told me.

When Dwayne had first joined the expedition years earlier, the risks of the climb had appeared to be relatively minimal. There had been few serious accidents on Everest in recent years, and it had looked like the Canadians could negotiate the icefall safely. "If I knew even one person would die," he said, "I wouldn't have come on this expedition. I came with reasonable hope there would be no deaths, but I knew it could be dangerous and I knew there could be. My friends have said it's Russian roulette to go up there, but I feel we can make mountaineering decisions on this climb and have a certain amount of safety. There's always that chance, anywhere you are in your life, you could get killed."

Dwayne sent a message down with the mail-runners to have his gear sent back. He was ready to stay.

Laurie, who was wrapped in bandages to protect his cracked ribs, found his own compelling reasons to continue. "I haven't given it my best yet," he told me. "The remaining problems are acceptable, the risks are acceptable. What faces us isn't a voodoo curse or anything like that. It's a classic mountaineering problem of icefall, avalanche-swept valley, logistics, and whether or not we're going to have the strength at high altitude to push for the summit."

He also had a gut feeling that if he backed away from the mountain, it would somehow be a waste of the lives of the men who had died. He was thinking not only of Blair and the Sherpas, but also of John Lauchlan, one of the climbers he most admired. Laurie felt compelled to stay, and he rationalized that the remaining team had the strength and skills to at least have a chance of success. "We've got an intelligent grasp of what's happening," he said as he looked back toward the icefall. "I certainly don't feel like I'm blindly throwing myself at the mountain. Not at all."

Pat felt the drive to continue as well, and he saw new possibilities with a fresh approach. The sheer size of the original expedition had created a juggernaut, from his perspective. At first, the strength in numbers had been an asset, but it had eventually proved to be the team's downfall. The top-down approach to leadership had gone against the grain of the seasoned climbers, who were much more comfortable with making decisions by consensus. With a smaller team, Pat saw the potential for improved communication. And with the loads already stashed at Camp 1, the climbers could concentrate on the upper mountain without exposing themselves to the perils of additional carries through the icefall.

Alan was one of the staunchest advocates of continuing. At one point, when Bill was talking about changing tactics and switching to a less demanding route, he suggested the possibility of folding the expedition if the team couldn't come up with a suitable plan. Al was outraged. "As far as I'm concerned, if we quit now, it's all politics," he stormed.

A New Beginning

He threatened to join the New Zealand expedition, suggesting that they would seek permission to switch from Lhotse and tackle the route the Canadians had abandoned. He was particularly incensed when John suggested that the expedition should consider the team's image and admit defeat in the interests of the corporate sponsors.

"The accidents have happened," Al maintained. "There's nothing you can do to change that. What would Blair want? I don't think he'd want us to just back off. I don't think he'd want us to take high risks … Some risks are higher than others, and providing you understand what those risks are, then it's moral. It's only immoral if you ask people to take risks they don't understand. This route is dangerous. We knew that before we came. It hasn't become more dangerous. It's just the same. If you apply your skills and knowledge, you can keep the risks to a minimum."

Al and Speedy quickly worked out a revised plan. Ironically, the departure of six climbers made the logistics much simpler. The expedition would switch back to the original plan for the South Col route — a more reasonable goal given the depleted ranks. With more than 100 loads already above the icefall, the remaining team could get by with only a few additional carries through the dangerous terrain.

"We should call it Team Phoenix," Dave Read said of the diminished group when it became clear that there was a solid commitment to continue. The image of the expedition rising out of the ashes had a certain appeal, but the climbers were ready to poke fun at themselves and settled on a less heroic nickname — the CRASS Expedition (Canadian Remnants Attempt on Sagarmatha's Summit).

After eight days of uncertainty, grief, anger, resentment, and frustration, there was time to relax, regroup, and prepare for a renewed effort on the mountain. We gathered in the cook tent with the Sherpas and New Zealanders for a night of singing and card playing. A 20-litre jug of sour, milky white chang soon disappeared, and we stumbled off to get some sleep. There was work to do in the morning.

Chapter 7
Leap of Faith

It was clearly the turning point for the expedition. There was a new sense of clarity among the climbers who stayed. And for the first time, there was a genuine feeling of solidarity on the mountain.

Nevertheless, a dark cloud continued to loom over the team. Though they were more than ready to focus on their renewed goal, the climbers still had to account for past mistakes. The accidents and turmoil that had occurred on Everest had elicited an incredible amount of criticism, speculation, and second-guessing. And the day-to-day media coverage of the Canadian expedition made it impossible to set the controversies aside.

A story out of Ottawa quoted anonymous mountain

experts who suggested the climb was one of Canada's biggest mountaineering mistakes. "The worst is definitely not behind them," one expert said. Another speculated that altitude sickness had weakened the leaders' abilities to make sound judgments.

Roger Marshall had returned to Canada shortly after being kicked off the expedition, and he was more than eager to criticize those who had dumped him. "I am outraged at the suggestion that the six who walked off had become afraid of the mountain. That is rubbish," he told a reporter in Vancouver. "I am sure that they have quit because they now have doubts about the judgment of the expedition leaders."

The climbers who remained on Everest, along with their families back home, were particularly incensed when they read the scathing criticisms levelled by Alex Witten-Hannah, who had been on Everest with the New Zealand expedition. The Canadians had "incompetent leadership" and were not mentally prepared for the expedition, Witten-Hannah told a reporter in Kathmandu. The New Zealander accused Bill of sleeping in on the morning of the avalanche and failing to send a crucial weather report down from Camp 1 in time to abort the carry. He also said that Bill had given up control on the mountain when Blair was killed, since the leader had gone down to the valley to attend the funeral service for the Sherpas.

These harsh pronouncements were bitterly resented by the climbers who stayed, and even by some of those who left. Witten-Hannah was not an official member of the New

Zealand expedition and had limited climbing experience. Some wondered how he had the nerve to be so critical. Tim Auger pointed out that Canadian team members had helped the New Zealander get through the icefall when he became separated from his companions and was stricken by altitude sickness.

Witten-Hannah's interpretation of events was disputed by the Canadian team on several points. Climbers argued against the implication that Bill had been negligent by sleeping through a scheduled early morning radio call. In hindsight, a 3 a.m. call might well have saved the three Sherpas from the avalanche, but Bill had conferred with the team the night before the carry and, while some members had questioned the decision, the weather check was set for 5 a.m.

Members of the team also maintained that Witten-Hannah had made an unfair assumption when he said the Sherpas who died had been sent ahead to clear the trail. In fact, Canadians had been out in front, and the sahibs and Sherpas had shared the risks through the icefall. Canadian climbers had been caught in the slide and could just as easily have been the ones who died.

In the scramble for news and instant analysis, a strange situation evolved. John Amatt had flown out to Kathmandu to act as spokesman for the team on the mountain. I was still in base camp sending back information from the mountainside. Back in Canada, competing newspapers and magazines were carrying stories based on interviews with spokesmen located in Montreal and Calgary. The news was coming from a variety of sources, and there was plenty of room for distortion. In base camp, climbers were disheartened and angered by the negative tone in many of the clippings mailed from home. They were frustrated when they saw errors or misinterpretations, but they also knew that the stories were already weeks old. It was almost impossible to forget about the team's image and just go ahead and do the job, trusting that the truth would eventually emerge.

The monsoon storms continued well into September, and the sahibs and Sherpas were anxious to begin the renewed attempt, to build momentum again and climb beyond their lingering doubts and uncertainties. There were jokes about the Canadian Everest Base Camp Expedition, but no one wanted to push too hard this time around. It was better to wait.

The climbers used the time for healing — some physically, some emotionally. Laurie trekked down to Pheriche with the hope that his ribs would heal more quickly at lower elevation. Bill left camp on September 10 to take a break from the relentless pressure. On the mountain, he refused to yield to his emotions. It was a mode of operation that allowed him to make tough decisions, but he could only keep it up for so long. Down below, there were reminders of the deaths — insurance details to handle, and meetings with relatives of the Sherpas — but there were also green valleys and friendly faces to bolster his inner reserves. Bill was seeking some form of spiritual renewal as well.

He planned to visit the lama at Pangboche to receive his blessing and a supply of new holy rice and charms to help reassure the Sherpas and himself.

On the same day that Bill left camp, Alan, Lloyd, and Pat attempted to break trail through the icefall again but quickly found themselves in waist-deep snow. They barely made it to the traverse before having to turn back. The snow continued to fall overnight and well into the next day. We wondered if fortune would ever be with us.

The monotony of waiting for the weather to break was relieved on the night of September 11, when we assembled for a gala dinner party held next door at the Catalan camp. It was a patriotic holiday, and our neighbours had gone all out to prepare a feast. There was quail, champagne, beer, cheese, smoked meat, lasagne, salad, and chocolate cake. The Catalans had suffered their own setbacks, most notably a massive rockfall that wiped out a large part of their route, and they were equally anxious to relieve the tension of a long expedition. There was dancing on the tables and singing late into the night.

Finally, on September 15, the weather broke and clear skies reappeared. Al, Lloyd, and Pat returned to the icefall on the morning of September 16, and after 10 hours of slogging through deep snow and rebuilding the route, they made their way to Camp 1. Bill, Dwayne, and the Sherpas carried a load through the following day. The team was starting to make progress again, and Camp 2 was soon established, complete with a portable car shelter that would serve as the mess tent.

Life on the mountain settled into a new routine. There were daily reports radioed down to base camp from the climbers up in the Western Cwm. From the mountainside, Peter Spear made morning and evening calls to Earth Station Kathmandu, the communications centre at the Everest Sheraton.

Laurie was still resting in Pheriche. The break had done wonders for him. His ribs were sore but mending, and he was gathering strength and resolve for the task ahead. He garnished almost every meal with garlic to speed the healing process.

Canadians and Sherpas had carried the last few loads through the Khumbu within days of the team's second start. Most of the Canadian climbers made just a single carry through the icefall, which was virtually unrecognizable from a month earlier. Ropes were buried in snow or torn from their anchors, and sturdy ladders that bridged crevasses were twisted by the immense power of the shifting ice. A few parts of the old fixed line were salvaged, but rolls and rolls of new rope were stretched again through the tangle. Bill made a point of going through the icefall three times to demonstrate his commitment to the climb — not only to the Canadians and the Sherpas, but to himself.

On September 22, Lloyd and Dave made their way up through the icefall to re-establish Camp 1. Like Bill, Lloyd had taken a few days' rest away from the mountain, and Dave had been resting in base camp to recover from a back injury and regain the drive needed to go on. When they arrived at Camp 1, they radioed down to tell us that the icefall was a mess and the route was literally falling apart. The climbers up above felt it was best to close the route and leave it unattended until the end of the expedition. This way, the network of ropes and bridges wouldn't need to be maintained, and the climbers could devote more energy to the upper part of the mountain. The strategy made sense to everyone except Steve Bezruchka, who was in base camp, and Laurie, who was making his way back from the tiny hospital in Kunde, near Pheriche, where he'd had his ribs treated.

When Laurie arrived at camp on September 23, he had a tense radio call with Bill.

"It's too dangerous," Bill said as he repeated his order that no one go through the icefall.

Laurie was not one to give up easily. When he was a teenager, he wanted to take an Outward Bound course, but his father thought it was too risky. Laurie decided to satisfy his taste for adventure by leaving home at 17 and becoming a merchant seaman. At 20, he finally enrolled in an Outward Bound course in Colorado and ended up working for the program.

While Bill didn't want to risk another death, he eventually relented under Laurie's persistence and agreed to let him take his chances alone in the icefall the following day. They made a pact that Laurie would check in regularly to give progress reports. Both knew that rescue was unlikely if something were to happen, but the progress reports would at least give the team a sense of where to look for the body.

Though Laurie was still feeling pain in his ribs, his time at lower altitude had given him a chance to rebuild his stamina. He set a quick pace and gingerly worked his way up the route — a route that had deteriorated even more, with warped bridges and ropes dislodged from their anchors. He pressed on steadily until he came to a 30-metre-deep crevasse. A ladder had been used to bridge the gap, but it had pulled loose on the far side. The aluminum span stuck out like a diving board, 1.5 metres short of the patch of ice that offered what passed for solid footing in the twisted maze.

When he was young, Laurie had been taunted by a schoolmate for not having any imagination because he'd had trouble drawing a picture. As he grew older, he realized that mountaineering offered the chance of creativity, and he soon knew that he'd found his "game." Laurie came to see climbing a big mountain as a little like stealing bases on a ball diamond. Like the bases, there are places on a mountain where there is momentary refuge before the next dash toward the final goal. "You try to make it to the summit and back down without being tagged out," he reasoned. "The only difference is that if you get tagged out on the mountain, usually you pay with your life."

Laurie looked for alternative ways to get around the chasm, but after an hour had passed, he calculated that it was just too risky. His Everest dream was over, and he turned to head back to base camp. Laurie had never looked at Everest as a mountain to conquer — it was a worthy goal that deserved respect. If there was something to conquer, it was his inner doubts and the self-imposed limitations that he saw as a cage. His experience told him he had made his best effort and there was no shame in turning back. Still, there was a faint voice inside his head that asked, "Have you given it more than your best?"

It was the kind of personal challenge that Laurie couldn't resist. He returned to the edge of the crevasse. The odds of leaping safely to the other side were 50-50 at best, he figured. He looked for ways to at least give himself a chance at survival in case he failed. Summoning his courage, he rigged Petzl ascender clamps to the rope that spanned the crevasse, inched his way to the end of the ladder, and leapt.

The distance of the jump was too great for Laurie to land on his feet, but he managed to swing his ice axe and get a tenuous grip on the edge of the ice wall on the far side of the crevasse. He kicked his crampons into the ice and slowly hauled himself up. Through the exhaustion and pain, he also began to gain a new sense of confidence. He had come up against big obstacles in the mountains before. Sometimes he'd failed to overcome these obstacles, but he'd always regarded failure as a "reconnaissance mission," another step toward eventual success. Only by continuing to try is there a chance of success, he reminded himself.

Laurie climbed on alone to Camp 1, then up to rejoin

the team at Camp 2. He felt that he had left many of his fears behind when he'd made his "leap of faith," but a sense of apprehension returned when he thought about having to face the man who had ordered the icefall closed. He was surprised and delighted when Bill rushed up to greet him at the high camp.

"It's great you're here," Bill told him, then went on to explain that while he hadn't wanted to ask Laurie to put himself at risk in the icefall, he had been in need of extra manpower and knew that Laurie's presence higher up the mountain would be a valuable addition. "Besides," he added with a grin, "I knew you'd come up no matter what."

Chapter 8
"We Have an Emergency"

With Laurie back in their ranks, the climbers settled into a rotation, with the strongest Canadians working alongside the best Sherpas in pushing the route, while others settled in behind hauling loads. There was a price to pay for the exertion, and after each foray, they had to take time off to rest and recover. Wind had become a major obstacle, whipping over the shoulder of Everest and blasting down onto the climbers. As ever, the rigours of altitude were also wearing the men down. They felt like they had aged 20 years. "You walk around like an old man, especially if you've got a load on your back," Bill said.

While Camp 2 was a tiny tent village spread out on a rocky stretch of the Western Cwm, Camp 3 amounted to just three box tents perched on a steep snow slope below the South Col. A small ice cliff up the mountain slope provided some protection from avalanches, and the tough outer shell of the tents offered a slim measure of insurance against rocks blown down from above. Clearly, Camp 3 was not a place to linger.

The clear, cold weather allowed for steady progress, and the team pushed up through the Yellow Band, a notoriously fragile layer of rock. With only crumbling limestone to secure the rope, a fall could be disastrous. Ever cautious, the team continued, and by the end of the month, they were close to the South Col.

By October 4, summit fever had spread through all the camps. Al Burgess, Sungdare, and Lhakpa Dorje had pushed the route up to the South Col the day before. Eleven Sherpas had followed them, dropping food and supplies on the gap at 7925 metres between Everest and Lhotse. Laurie, Dave, and Lloyd were designated to move into position for a summit bid on October 5. The two strongest Canadians would join up with Sungdare and Lhakpa Dorje to push for the top.

While it looked like success was within reach, the climbing conditions continued to test the limits of the Canadians and Sherpas. Laurie had gone ahead of Dave and Lloyd, and he struggled to make his way up to the South Col as the temperature dropped to –25 degrees Celsius and the winds gusted up to 100 kilometres an hour — powerful enough to knock him down flat on the frozen mountainside.

His face was scarred by ice crystals blown down at high

velocity, and his hood kept sliding off his head. He felt like he was in a war zone as the wind gusted across Lhotse and the South Col, stripping off pieces of ice that crashed below like mortar shells.

At times, blowing snow and ice cut visibility to barely 10 metres, and he would crouch into a ball to protect himself. It was a mixed blessing when he could actually see what he'd gotten himself into. Huge chunks of ice were flung into the air hundreds of metres above, and he watched as they hit the slopes and cartwheeled down the mountain. Small pieces the size of fists were continuously hitting his body. As he inched his way upward, he saw rocks big enough to do some serious damage imbedded in the snow and ice. He knew that they, too, had been blown down from above, and that he had to be vigilant.

As Laurie tried to push his way up to the Col, the thin air was gradually taking its toll. With almost no energy left, he was barely making progress — forcing himself a few metres upward, then breathing deeply for two or three minutes before going a few metres more.

Exhausted and chilled to the bone, Laurie arrived at the South Col with Sungdare and Lhakpa Dorje just after noon on October 4. By 2 p.m., they had established their camp, and with the help of hot drinks, they gradually regained their strength. It was calm and surprisingly mild as the trio sorted out their equipment and waited for Dave and Lloyd to show up.

By late afternoon, Dave and Lloyd still hadn't arrived at

the South Col. Both men were out of radio contact, but their teammates assumed that the pair had had trouble adjusting to the altitude and had turned back. Bill was still confident that Laurie could push on with the Sherpas, but he remained cautious. "Laurie, this might be our only chance at the summit," Bill radioed from Camp 2. "I want you to take great care. If there's any doubt, I want you to come back. I don't want to lose you. I think you realize how important it is. You're in a fantastic position. We all wish we were with you now."

Laurie sounded self-assured when he replied from Camp 4. "Don't worry about me. I'm feeling good. I'm not into pushing it and losing my feet or my hands or my fingers and toes. You don't have to worry about that. I worry about you, Bill, because if I don't come back, my girlfriend's going to kill you, so we both have a vested interest."

Though Laurie was looking forward to embarking on the final push the next day, his eagerness was tempered with growing concern. It was getting dark, and Dave and Lloyd were still missing. Bill radioed up to Laurie. "If Dave or Lloyd reach you at Camp 4, I don't think they should go to the summit. They are too slow. This is a direct order not to go to the summit."

A few minutes later, it looked like Laurie wouldn't get a chance, either. "Laurie, we have an emergency. We have an emergency," Bill said.

Everyone who overheard the radio call was gripped with the sudden fear that members of the team were again in grave danger. In a calm voice, Bill told Laurie that Dave and Lloyd were apparently still pushing for the Col and that Lloyd was having trouble with his oxygen system. Laurie had been preparing to brew his final cup of tea and get some rest for the day ahead, but he and the Sherpas quickly formed a rescue party to descend and look for the missing pair. Pat Morrow and Dwayne Congdon, meanwhile, began climbing up to Camp 3 with sleeping bags and other emergency gear in case they needed to evacuate either of the men.

From the start of the expedition, Laurie had been careful not to think too much about his own chances of reaching the summit. But after having arrived at the Col, he had finally allowed himself to consider the possibility that he might reach the top. And now, almost instantly, it seemed like the opportunity was being taken away. If the summit team used up too much oxygen in the search for Dave and Lloyd, Laurie would have to return to a lower camp, and someone else would get his turn. At that point, it was the luck of the draw.

Just as the summit team was ready to descend from Camp 4, Dave Read slogged the final few steps up onto the Col. Laurie couldn't understand why Dave had pushed himself to exhaustion instead of turning back. He didn't know that Dave had set the Col as his own personal goal for the expedition and was determined to reach it. "That's my Everest," Dave said with satisfaction as he gradually recovered from his exhausting ascent.

Now the concern was focused entirely on Lloyd. He was three weeks from his 43rd birthday and the senior member of the expedition. He was also my next-door neighbour in Canmore. I was thrilled when I first heard that he had a chance at the summit, but now I worried that he had pushed himself too hard and fallen prey to the mountain. Lloyd had been picked as a summit candidate since he, like Laurie, had not gone back to altitude as quickly as the others. Most of the climbers had spent 18 days above base camp, and their energy reserves were running low. Lloyd, who had spent only 13 days in the upper camps, was not as worn down. Al Burgess, who had done much of the hard work in pushing the route up to the Col, was also considered a prime contender for the summit honour, but he needed to rest.

As deputy leader, Lloyd had been a perfect complement to Bill. While Bill was outspoken and abrasive at times, Lloyd was quiet and diplomatic. When Bill was prepared for confrontation, Lloyd was more open to compromise and negotiation. After the accidents, he favoured ending the expedition but backed Bill and the others when they decided to stay. More importantly, he'd made his own decision that the route could be tackled in relative safety. "My wife knows me well enough to know I wouldn't take any unnecessary risks," he'd said. But to those of us waiting anxiously for news of Lloyd's whereabouts late on October 4, it looked like he might have been wrong: the mountain might have been too dangerous.

As it turned out, Lloyd himself hadn't been particularly worried about his safety that day. He had been cursing his bad luck. For the final push, he had chosen a sophisticated breathing regulator that supplied bottled oxygen in limited amounts with each inhalation. Laurie had picked a bulkier and older system with a regulator that fed a constant flow of oxygen into his mask. It was less efficient but there was less that could go wrong.

Lloyd's system soon broke down between Camp 3 and 4, and he spent an hour fiddling with the mechanism before deciding to abandon it and push up to the Col without an oxygen tank. He knew there would be two extra bottles at Camp 4 that he could use for the summit attempt. As darkness descended, he was still making slow progress. Then he saw two oxygen bottles sticking out in the snow beside the frozen footsteps up the mountainside, and, with a sinking feeling, he knew he wouldn't get a chance at the summit. One of the Sherpas hadn't been able to carry the load all the way to Camp 4, which meant there was no extra oxygen for a fourth member of the summit team. Lloyd could try carrying the 15-kilogram tanks himself, but he'd already been out 12 hours, and much harder terrain still lay ahead. He had the Canadian flag in his pack, ready to place it on the summit, but now he knew someone else would have to make the final push.

To add to his frustration, Lloyd learned that his misfortune might cost Laurie his chance at the summit as well. He could hear the concern of Bill and the other team members in a static-filled transmission over his portable radio. But there was too much interference from an outcrop of rock for him to radio back. As he continued to listen to his radio,

Lloyd heard that the climbers in Camp 4 were getting ready to look for him. He knew that if they got very far, they would be too burned out to go back up for a summit attempt.

Summoning his last reserve of energy, Lloyd descended quickly, making repeated attempts to reach the rest of the team by radio. After 300 metres of hasty down-climbing, he managed to contact Camp 2 and tell them he was on his way down. The search was over. The message was relayed up to Laurie, Dave, and the Sherpas, and they settled in to prepare for the day's work ahead.

Laurie readied his pack and brewed yet another pot of tea — he was drinking six or seven litres of fluid a day to ward off dehydration and altitude sickness. He left a little brew to freeze in the container on the hanging stove (so it could be quickly heated in the morning) and filled a thermos that he slipped into his sleeping bag. Next he took out his boot liners and stuffed them with his woollen mitts to remove the moisture. And finally, he put on his oxygen mask and set the flow at two for the little amount he needed to sleep. It was 11 p.m. He and the Sherpas would be setting out in five hours. Lying there, in his down-filled cocoon, he was alone with his thoughts and his doubts.

It could have been any member of the team in his place, he knew. Ironically, his injury had helped his chances. It had given him a little more time at low altitude before the second push. But now was he risking too much, relying too much on an oxygen system that could freeze up and leave him gasping? He'd wanted to reach the South Col without using oxygen tanks. That way, he would have known for certain that there was some margin of safety, that he had acclimatized well enough to have a strong chance of survival in case he ran out of supplementary air. But he had turned on his oxygen system a few hundred metres below the South Col to ease his progress and save some energy. Had it been a mistake to disregard his own measure of readiness? Dave assured him that it wasn't a question of going for a high-altitude mark without oxygen. The summit was the main goal.

At 3 a.m., Laurie got up and reheated his tea. He slowly dressed and checked his gear. Even the simple task of getting his double boots on seemed to take an eternity. Not only was the altitude clouding his thought process, his hands were swollen and aching from all the cuts and scrapes that simply wouldn't heal in the harsh environment.

Two hours' sleep. That's all he'd managed, and he'd had little more the night before. He asked the Sherpas about going for the summit with so little rest. Sungdare, who had already been to the top of Everest twice, said it was okay to go one or two nights without sleep, but anything more was pushing it.

As he waited for the Sherpas to get ready, Laurie checked the weather. It was –34 degrees Celsius and the winds were light. For the Himalayas, the conditions were ideal.

When dawn broke clear and calm on October 5, Laurie, Sungdare, and Lhakpa Dorje were already well on their way to the summit. They had started out at 4:15 a.m. Dave had considered joining them in the attempt but realized there wasn't enough oxygen and he might jeopardize the others if he tried. He drew a happy face on Laurie's bright yellow oxygen bottle and sent him out with the battle cry, "Rock on."

Sungdare set a demanding pace from the start, and Laurie cranked up his oxygen system to eight so he could keep up. The 25-year-old Sherpa was moving well in the lead. Laurie was worried about running out of oxygen in an effort to maintain that speed.

There was virtually no room for error. The three climbers were roped together for safety, but if one fell and the other two couldn't brake his fall, they would all have a long ride down. The Sherpas were adept at moving quickly, but Laurie wasn't sure they had a high enough regard for the dangerous terrain. Every time he took a step, he kicked his feet twice and put in his axe up to the hilt. "I don't want to make a mistake," he kept telling himself.

The early light brought magnificent views, but there was no time to take in the scenery. With his bulky oxygen mask and the goggles he was wearing to shield his eyes from the blinding sunlight, it was all Laurie could do to watch where he was placing his feet. "Nothing complicated, simple mountaineering," he reminded himself over and over again.

When the trio was less than two hours out, about a third of the way to the summit, Laurie had to stop. He had been using the French technique of kicking steps at an angle on the hard green-blue ice. The twisting motion had cut the circulation of blood to his feet, and his right foot was painfully cold. His instincts were clear. Don't ignore it. It won't go away. People lose their feet for doing things like that. Be patient. Get control of the situation.

Laurie took off his plastic double boot and socks and warmed his foot with both hands. The Sherpas drank tea, but Laurie didn't want to take his hands off his foot. He knew he was taking a chance by not drinking. After a few minutes, his foot was comfortable and he laced up his boot more loosely this time. They set off again at the same brisk pace.

As the sun began to rise above the vast Tibetan plateau, the climbers trudged up past a frozen windswept mound that seemed strangely out of place. Sungdare instantly recognized it. The realization came slower to the others. It was the German woman.

Sungdare had first reached the summit of Everest while working on the ill-fated 1979 German expedition. He and American guide Ray Genet reached the top on October 2 in an epic push with Hannelore Schmatz, wife of the expedition leader. Schmatz became the fourth woman to reach the summit, and, at 39, the oldest. But after reaching the top, she was simply too exhausted to make the trip back down. The trio was forced to bivouac without oxygen just a few hundred metres below the summit. Genet died during the night, and Schmatz perished soon after, becoming the first woman to die on Everest. Sungdare, who had stayed with Schmatz until the end, lost several toes to the cold. Despite the offer of a reward and pleas from her husband that other climbers retrieve Schmatz's body, the task proved too difficult. She has remained on the mountain as a solemn reminder of the danger of pushing too hard for the summit.

By 8 a.m., Laurie, Sungdare, and Lhakpa Dorje had reached the South Summit — just 300 metres from their goal. Laurie's thoughts were concentrated on the long, sharp edge leading to the summit. Huge windslabs of snow were perched along the way. When Sungdare stepped onto one crusty section, part of it broke off and sailed silently into the distance. Soon after that, Laurie punched his axe into the snow along the ridge and was startled to see daylight down below. The climbers were on a cornice, a windblown patch of snow that was hanging over the side of the rock. It was a potential trap, but the trio was moving quickly and smoothly.

The main climbing obstacle was a short, steep pitch of broken rock known as the Hillary Step. It is only a few metres high and at sea level would be no challenge at all. But in the rarefied air, and after weeks of exhausting work, the climbers had to take it slowly and carefully. Each step, each hold with their axes was crucial. Through the cold and exhaustion, Laurie had to maintain his focus, maintain concentration, maintain control. The rhythm continued: take a step, pound in the ice axe, take three breaths, then one more step.

He later recalled that a remarkable sense of calm came over him as he neared the top. "There were no great thoughts about whether I was going to make it or I wasn't going to make it. Aside from the small doubts that came through my mind as I was going up, there was the comforting feeling of the wave of support and effort that had gone into this expedition over the past two months. It's hard to put into words, but it felt like I was being floated to the summit, that yes, there was a chance we might not make it, the slope was steep and my feet were freezing and I didn't have the strength that I normally have because I'd gotten worn down and everything. It wasn't like those thoughts of not making it weren't there, but the general feeling inside was that all the effort, all the blood that had been shed up until this day was going to get me to the top regardless of what I had to do.

"It was like every step that I took upward was justification for all the work, blood, and sweat that had gone into this trip."

As Laurie forced himself to concentrate on precise technique, Sungdare, framed in brilliant sunshine, stopped without warning, turned, raised a clenched fist, and shouted "Hey-ey." The salute had become a joke among the climbers. Dave and Laurie had started it during the early stages of the expedition, when they were slogging up the mountainside humping loads to higher camps and then returning exhausted to their tents below. They knew they weren't fooling anyone when they mustered enough strength to give their "hard men" salute, but they continued to do it all the same.

Sungdare had picked up the gesture, and now he was

raising his arm above the highest point on the earth. Laurie's boot broke through the snow cover, and he fell to one knee as he struggled for the summit. Then, in a moment that was impossible to truly imagine, he was standing there, on a wind-blasted patch of snow-covered rock, a majestic perch no bigger than a tabletop.

As soon as Lhakpa Dorje joined them, Laurie began to savour the view. Off in the distance, the horizon showed the distinct curve of the planet. "I can see forever, not a cloud in the sky," Laurie thought. To the north, the Rongbuk Glacier snaked off in the distance, surrounded by peaks rising from the Tibetan plateau. Laurie took special satisfaction in looking across the Western Cwm, down on the summit of Nuptse, the mountain that had defeated the Canadians on a training climb just a year earlier.

The Sherpas unfurled their small Nepalese flag while Laurie took photograph after photograph. There was no Canadian flag to display. Lloyd had been designated to carry it as part of the summit team. When he was forced back, the flag had stayed with him.

Laurie's summit was the culmination of years of planning and preparation, as well as personal sacrifices and occasional dreams of success. But Laurie wouldn't allow himself the luxury of taking this all in. He knew that the descent is often the deadliest part of a climb, because mountaineers are tempted to let down their guard after achieving their main goal. But the paramount goal, of course, is returning safely, and Laurie reminded himself of the basic precautions he still needed to take.

As they descended from the summit, the trio retraced their steps, taking the same route down that they had travelled on the way up. Laurie soon grew impatient with Lhakpa Dorje's slow pace on the descent and was tempted to take off his rope and move more quickly on his own. He was just about to untie when he fell into a crevasse up to his waist. He got out, took two more steps, and fell into another. It was as if the mountain was offering a gentle reminder that climbers should never let their guard down.

Back at base camp, anticipation was building as we anxiously awaited word from the summit team. At noon, the radio began to crackle with static, and then we heard Laurie's raspy voice. "Camp 4 to base camp. How do you copy?"

"Base camp to Camp 4. We copy you loud and clear."

"Well copy this. We did it!" Laurie shouted.

There were whoops of joy from camps up and down the mountain.

As Laurie sipped tea at Camp 4 and prepared for the final descent, his thoughts turned to Blair. "I was hoping he was proud of us, those few of us that continued. I felt that when he was with us, he was proud of being with us, glad of being with this type of people, and he was happy in his work. The last images I have of Blair are of his laughter and of him joking."

Chapter 9
Remembrance

The jubilation on the mountain quickly spread back to Kathmandu and Canada. Messages of congratulations began to flood into the communication centre at the Everest Sheraton. Still, the Nepalese bureaucrats were as vigilant as ever. Prime Minister Pierre Trudeau and Governor General Edward Schreyer attempted to establish a radio link to talk to the mountaineers directly, but our liaison officer said the calls would have to be cleared first by the tourism ministry. John Amatt was outraged, but he agreed to go through proper channels. Unfortunately, the calls never happened. It was just too hard to coordinate the schedules of the government leaders back home with the brief windows of opportunity for good radio signals to base camp.

The climbers who were still on the mountain felt a renewed sense of energy after the first success. The weather was still holding, and they were ready to make at least one more attempt before coming down for good.

On October 6, Al, Dwayne, Lloyd, Pat, and a group of Sherpas set out from Camp 2 to the South Col. As the strongest climber, Al was designated as the prime candidate to stay at Camp 4 and push for the summit with Lhakpa Tshering and Pema Dorje, two young but very strong Sherpas.

Pat was going along with his 35-millimetre cameras and a video camera to record as much of the ascent as possible. He also had a personal objective in mind. "Throughout the whole expedition, my main goal was to make it to the South Col, 'cause it makes good party talk," he told me later.

Lloyd was still a potential summiteer as well, but after the long push up to Camp 4, he realized he'd reached his limit. Dwayne, meanwhile, was determined to reach the Col without using oxygen tanks in order to prove to himself that he could acclimatize well enough to reach the summit. He slowly made his way up to the high camp and succeeded in doing it without using the tanks that he carried. However, the effort took too much out of him to consider a summit attempt the following day. (It would take four more years, but that investment of energy would finally pay off when the experience and confidence he earned in 1982 helped Dwayne reach the summit during Canada's second and much more ambitious attempt of Everest.)

Pat and Al both used oxygen masks on their way to the Col to save their strength. Pat decided to use Laurie's constant flow mask and regulator since it had already proven itself at altitude. Al chose the more finicky but supposedly more efficient diluter-demand model. His mistake was evident well below the Col. No matter how much he fiddled with the flow regulator, precious little oxygen was released.

Despite his struggles with the oxygen mask, Al kept pushing up to the Col. He was surprised when he took off the mask and instantly felt much better. Not only was the mask not feeding him extra oxygen, it was restricting his breathing of the already thin natural air. Upon reaching Camp 4, he tried to mend his regulator and rig a mask using parts he'd salvaged from high on the mountain.

The South Col has become one of the world's highest junkyards. Teams that struggle to ferry food and equipment farther and farther up the mountain have much less interest in spending time carrying surpluses back down when it's all over. Huge mounds of mainly empty oxygen bottles are strewn across the Col. Plenty of tanks are half full or better. One Polish expedition was so confident of finding salvageable oxygen bottles at the Col that they simply brought along regulators and didn't have to carry tanks with them to their high camp.

Al fiddled with several kinds of regulators and masks before finally giving up and trying to get some rest without artificial air. Pat's luck was decidedly different. When he reached the high camp, he took off his mask and felt surprisingly invigorated. He immediately revised his goal and decided to accompany Al and the Sherpas to the south summit, where he could turn back and safely descend on his own. His oxygen system continued to work well, but he had his own problems getting to sleep. The inflated Thermarest sleeping pad in his tent had been punctured by crampons. He had to settle into his sleeping bag with no extra padding between his weary body and the row of empty oxygen bottles that he'd placed on his tent floor for ballast.

It was 5:15 a.m., October 7, when Al, Pat, Pema Dorje, and Lhakpa Tshering set out. The Sherpas were ready and eager. "They set off like bloody rockets. They kept going faster and faster," Al later recalled.

Pat quickly realized he couldn't match their pace and untied himself from the rope that joined the summit team. As the trio moved quickly up a slope of 40-degree snow and ice, Al knew he hadn't been able to get his oxygen system functioning. "I realized this bastard system hadn't been working. I felt as if somebody had put a wet towel around my face."

Once again, he felt relief when he ripped the faulty mask from his face. As he and the Sherpas fiddled with the system, Al realized that his options were limited. "I wasn't going to drag the [oxygen] system from Pat's neck," Al said later in base camp. "I mean, what could I say?"

Al thought about continuing on without oxygen, but he knew how much energy it would take to climb in the rarefied air and doubted that he would have enough strength left to descend safely. He also could not justify asking the Sherpas to give up one of their oxygen systems so that he could go on. Al felt a strong affinity for Pema Dorje and Lhakpa Tshering and didn't want to take away either of their chances for the summit.

Unwilling to ask the others to give up their oxygen systems, and aware enough to realize the risk of going without a mask, Al chose to turn back. He was disappointed not only because his oxygen system had failed, but also because he had become so physically worn down that he didn't feel able to make the attempt without the aid of tanks and a breathing system.

Pat, who seemed to gain energy as the morning wore on, had passed the trio and was resting 100 metres up the slope. He had started to sense that the summit was possible and was determined to go as far as he could. After being worn down by weeks of exhausting work high on Everest, he began to feel that the mountain was somehow returning the energy. Pat knew he would likely have the only remaining chance at the summit for this expedition. It simply added to the flow of adrenalin. "I was really stimulated. It was like I was carrying the ball at that point. I felt I was working okay, my system was working okay."

Lhakpa Tshering and Pema Dorje reluctantly said good-bye to Al and worked their way up to Pat, where they roped up and set their sights on the summit. The Sherpas could barely contain their excitement, and Pat marvelled at their enthusiasm, comparing them to a couple of high-energy kids.

Pat led the way, following the windblown tracks from two days earlier. The bulky oxygen masks interfered with the trio's darkened goggles. Pat tried to make do with reduced vision, but Pema Dorje kept lifting his goggles and squinting in the bright Himalayan sunshine. It was a mistake that would soon blind him for days and nearly cost him his life.

The small group moved slowly but steadily upwards, pausing briefly by the body of Hannelore Schmatz and taking their time to cautiously move up the crumbling face of the Hillary Step. "Rotten snow, rotten rock," Pat said to himself as he surveyed the eight-metre obstacle.

On the long summit ridge, Pat captured frame after frame as he took particular photographer's delight in the crisp, clear air.

At 11:30 a.m., the threesome reached the summit and stood arm-in-arm on top of the world. For Pat, the exhilaration was like the first time he had reached a mountaintop in the Rockies. But like Laurie, he quickly focused his attention on the tasks at hand. He took as many shots as possible and had Pema Dorje take his picture. Pat's pose looked deceptively composed, with a bare hand holding his ice axe and the oxygen mask dropped away from his face. He didn't hold the pose long. "When you were without oxygen it was like being in a vacuum. Six seconds, and you were close to unconscious."

Just as the trio was about to start back down, the Sherpas told Pat they had forgotten to bring an offering. Pat reached inside a pocket and produced a Kit Kat chocolate bar — snack food for the gods.

As they made their descent along the narrow ridge, Pat realized extreme caution would be needed with Pema Dorje, who was stumbling because of his impaired vision. Twice he slipped and fell. Twice, Pat and Lhakpa Tshering saw it coming and dug their ice axes into the snow to brake his fall and keep from being pulled from the mountainside.

In base camp, the sense of jubilation after the first summit success had again given way to apprehension as we waited to hear from the second summit team. We were starting to pack up gear and think about heading home, but we rarely strayed far from the communications tent.

At 2 p.m., Pat's deadpan voice came over the base camp radio from Camp 4. "There's nothing up there but snow and rock, nothing to get very excited about."

He may have been trying to conceal his own excitement, but there was no attempt to keep a lid on the joy elsewhere on the mountain. We hugged one another in camp and relayed congratulations up and down the route.

But, with the end of the expedition in sight and a longing for the comforts of home, no one was inclined to linger. The evacuation of the mountain was swift. Sherpas, who knew they could keep whatever they scrounged from the camps, crammed their packs and hauled loads of 50 kilograms or more. The vow of cleaning off the mountain was quickly abandoned by climbers weary from weeks at high altitude. Some equipment was hastily stashed in crevasses, while other gear was left to blow in the wind. Pat tried to salvage one of the bulky high-altitude sleeping bags by tossing it down from Camp 4, hoping to retrieve it somewhere in the Western Cwm. No doubt, it is still up there somewhere.

As the climbers neared the base of the mountain, they still had one final obstacle. None took it lightly. The Sherpas gave Laurie sacred rice to sprinkle as an offering to the Khumbu Icefall.

The route through the maze of ice had turned into a nightmare in the weeks since the Canadians and high-altitude Sherpas had moved up the mountain for the duration. Ropes were stretched and broken. Sturdy aluminum ladders were further twisted and contorted. Spans of ladders that had bridged crevasses were now dangling in mid-air, suspended precariously by dislodged anchor ropes. It was a reminder for Laurie of the gaping chasm that had almost ended his role on the expedition. He and his teammates knew that their success in reaching the summit did not give them any guarantee of a safe return. They were anxious to get off the mountain, and it was a challenge to take the time to pound in new anchors and secure ropes and bridges for the final journey through the fateful terrain. They knew that two men remained buried under the snow and ice that they had to cross, and Blair was in their thoughts as they climbed down past the blocks of ice that had proven to be a deadly trap.

Those of us in base camp crossed the well-worn trail to

the foot of the icefall and offered juice, beer, and whiskey to climbers who were exuberant and relieved to be safe at last. Team members embraced and shouted. Many were on the verge of tears as it sank in that all their tension and anxiety could be left behind on the mountain. Dave Read took a long swig of orange juice and proclaimed that it was just like champagne after the days of struggle and hardships.

Bill was more relieved than anyone. He dropped his stoic mask as he took alternate swigs from a mug of tea and a tumbler of Seagram's whiskey. "The thing about Everest is it doesn't let up," he said to me. "Everything is so strung out, you don't relax. I knew if I blew it, there was no leeway, no margin. Once we made a commitment to go on, we had to climb the mountain, not have any deaths or screw-ups and get down safely. That is a really hard line. It really is. For the last month now, I've been sitting on a razor edge with a sore ass."

Base camp cleared out quickly as climbers began the short trek to an airstrip at Lukla for the 45-minute flight back to Kathmandu and a celebration that included Thanksgiving turkey. As we reached the sacred ridge above Dughla, each of us carried a rock to the pile that a Sherpa craftsman would later turn into a stone memorial for Blair. His marker stands next to the chortens for the three Sherpas, Pasang Sona, Ang Tsultim, and Dawa Dorje.

Bill felt deep pride in the mountaineers who remained on Everest to climb the mountain in honour of those who died.

"Their remembrance is that we didn't walk away," he said.

Epilogue

Laurie Skreslet continues to climb in the world's tallest mountain ranges. He uses his experiences in the mountains to inspire everyone from corporate leaders to schoolchildren to take risks in their lives and push themselves to greater achievements.

Pat Morrow kept his spirit of adventure alive with his successful quest to reach the highest peak on each of the seven continents. He returns frequently to the Himalayas and other exotic locales to produce documentaries that highlight the strength of the human spirit.

Roger Marshall turned to the risky challenge of solo high-altitude climbing and scaled Kangchenjunga, the world's third tallest peak, in 1984. In May 1987, he died making his second solo attempt on Everest.

Bill March returned to teaching outdoor pursuits at the University of Calgary. On September 8, 1990, Bill was hiking a scenic trail in the Purcell Mountains of British Columbia when he collapsed and died of natural causes. He had been planning to write a book about the challenges of leadership.

Jim Elzinga was determined to return to Everest with a cohesive team and a more inclusive leadership style. In 1986, he led Everest Light, a team that included Everest '82 veterans Laurie Skreslet, James Blench, Dwayne Congdon, and Dave McNab. The expedition was a significant achievement. The climbers scaled the challenging West Ridge Route, with Congdon and Sharon Wood reaching the summit. Sharon became the first North American woman to stand atop Everest.

About two dozen Canadians are now among the approximately 2000 mountaineers who have reached the summit of Everest. Climbers continue to try to establish firsts — the youngest, the oldest, the speediest. The top can get to be a very crowded place, but every once in a while there is a reminder that there is still room for heroism and courage. In May 2006, Calgarian Andrew Brash was just 200 metres from the summit when he abandoned his attempt so that he could rescue an Australian mountaineer. Lincoln Hall had become delirious just after reaching the summit and was near death after spending the night alone at 8700 metres.

Brash's humanitarian efforts were justly hailed around the world, especially since they came just a week after a British climber perished on the mountain while 40 adventurers passed by in their misguided quest for glory.

Acknowledgments

Just as an expedition requires the support of many, so does a book about mountaineering. I am grateful to the members of the 1982 Canadian Mount Everest Expedition for allowing me to be part of that grand adventure and sharing their thoughts and feelings during and after such an intense experience. I particularly appreciated the reflections of Pat Morrow, Laurie Skreslet, Bill March, and Jim Elzinga.

As always, the encouragement from my immediate and extended family has helped me to meet my goals.

I would also like to thank Ted Giles of Detselig Enterprises, who published *Canadians on Everest*. That 1990 account formed the basis for this retelling as part of the Amazing Stories series.

My editor for this book at Altitude Publishing, Jill Foran, offered valuable feedback and suggestions, which I greatly appreciate.

About the Author

Bruce Patterson is the author of *Canadians on Everest* and Altitude's *Alberta SuperGuide*. He is co-author of Altitude's *Wild West SuperGuide*. After years of writing about outdoor adventures in the Canadian Rockies, he moved west to Vancouver Island, where he lives with his wife, Joan Wagner. He is arts editor of the *Victoria Times Colonist* newspaper.

Photo Credits